A Childhood on Steuben Street

A Historical Biography

By

DONALD FRANCIS OVEREND

Palmetto Publishing Group
Charleston, SC

A Childhood on Steuben Street
Copyright © 2018 by Donald Francis Overend

All rights are reserved. Except as authorize under United State Copyright laws, no portions of this book may be reproduced in any form without written permission from the author.

Printed in the United States of America

Library of Congress Cataloging in Publication Number: TXu 2-104-204
ISBN-13: 978-1-64111-380-9
ISBN-10: 1-64111-380-4

DEDICATION

This book is dedicated to my grandchildren Christopher, Mark, Teresa, Robert, April, Alex and Alyson along with my great grandchildren Michael and Evelyn.

INTRODUCTION

We are aware that as time passes life is ever changing. Traditions we once enjoyed will dwindle and perhaps even disappear forever. Loved ones we were surrounded by in our youth will pass on from this life leaving a residue of precious memories.

New generations will be born. Times will ever be changing. New inventions will evolve and overtake societies. New ideas will perpetuate and threaten traditional values including family attachments.

This writing will take readers back to the boyhood era experienced by the author. You will travel back to simpler days when families worked and played together, where education was a privilege and discipline was taught and strictly adhered to.

You will traverse an era before television, stereophonic sounds, air conditioners, fast food chains, computers, cell phones, video players, and many additional items found in use today.

Also, you will find that heating your home was much more involved that walking over to a wall and turning up a knob, operating and maintaining an automobile was much more tedious, and most people walked or rode a bus.

Very few homes had driveways since most people could not afford owning a vehicle. Neighbors looked after each other, watched over children at play, and responded quickly to resolve any episodes of mischief.

Now, find yourself a quiet seat, relax, and begin your journey back to a childhood on Steuben Street.

THE BUNGALOW

It was during February of 1946 that my parents were making preparations to move from our small one-bedroom home in the country. I recall sitting in my high chair watching the new owner's kitchen stove being delivered. Our cast iron stove had already been moved to our new home located in the city on Steuben Street. We were moving to the north side of Syracuse and into a much larger home within walking distance to a school. It was a strange feeling for me to be leaving a country setting, sandbox, lawn swing, and vegetable garden.

The home we were leaving behind was built by my father during World War II. Mom and Dad had purchased a double lot on Hopkins Road about one-half mile from Old Liverpool Road in Liverpool, New York. The lot had a single car garage on it and nothing else. During war time, construction materials were virtually impossible to obtain so Dad moved the garage forward and started converting it to a house. He jacked the garage up and built a floor under it. The garage had a front gable roof from which he constructed a saltbox type of structure to extend the roof area over a small addition. The area in the addition became the kitchen, bathroom, and rear entry. The converted garage was laid out to be a small parlor, single bedroom, and stairway to a very tiny attic.

No waterlines were available on Hopkins Road the first winter we lived there. Dad had to haul glass gallon jugs of water from Louke's Dairy located down on the nearest corner. The winter was particularly bad and Dad had to stay overnight on occasion at his Aunt Lizzie Greenfield's home on Park Street. As my sister and I approached school age the decision was made to move closer in to Syracuse.

Darkness had fallen by the time we piled into our 1936 Chevrolet Sedan and drove to the Steuben Street house that was to be our new home. Dad parked part way down the very narrow driveway. We walked up the front steps, down the side porch, and in the sitting room door. Mom instructed my sister and I to stay in one place until they found the light switch. The next thing I remember is my mother complaining about the previous owners taking all the light bulbs with them. She scurried through some of our packed boxes and located a bulb. The only light in the sitting room consisted of a wire drop with a bulb socket hanging from the center of the ceiling. As a matter of fact all the rooms that had lights were similar cord drops - no light fixtures as we know them today.

It was not until the next day that I got a glimpse of the exterior and I was pleasantly surprised that this was our new home. The Steuben Street bungalow was located approximately in the middle of the block. A large elm tree stood majestically in front between the sidewalk and street curb. The house was built in the year 1900 and provided about eleven-hundred square feet of interior space. Glancing up and down the street revealed other houses of all shapes and sizes nested closely together. A few had driveways while many others did not.

Our Steuben Street house was a bungalow by design. It was constructed on a cement block basement and had a front gable roof. A covered porch ran fully across the front of the house and extended around the driveway side for an additional fifteen feet. The front porch had a pent roof with a ceiling while the side porch was nested below the overhang of the gable roof. Turned wood posts were spaced along both porches to support the roof. Upper and lower rails interconnected between the posts. The rails were augmented with evenly spaced turned balusters that provided the waist high rails with an artistic flair. The area beneath the porch was skirted with wood lattice.

The driveway side of the house had a smaller twenty-four square foot porch with ceiling nested beneath an overhang of the gable roof. This porch provided a sheltered entry into a back room just off the kitchen area.

The main gable roof was covered with green diamond-shaped asphalt locking shingles whereas the front porch roof was overlaid with matching green rolled roofing paper. The porch posts, rails, and house trim was painted a flat brown color.

Although the house was sided in wood, Dad updated the outside by installing a dark red brick color stucco siding. He did this to achieve better weather insulation. Many homes back then used this type of siding and it helped immensely to control drafts during the winter months.

The house interior could be accessed via doors at four different locations, three on the main floor and one at the basement landing. A door on the front porch that was used very little allowed access into the parlor. The door around the corner on the front side porch was the entry point to the sitting room, the largest room in the house. The small rear side porch door was the entrance way into the back room. One last door on the far back corner of the house led to the cellar landing.

The parlor was at the very front of the house. It was a modest size room with a doorway leading to a small bedroom. A large open doorway on the back end of the parlor was the threshold into the sitting room. Two additional rooms sat adjacent to the sitting room. One was a bedroom that accommodated two twin beds. The other was a walk-in clothes closet.

The next room back from the sitting room was the kitchen. Directly off the kitchen were three more rooms, a bedroom, bathroom, and the back room that met the rear of the house. The bungalow also had a cellar and attic, neither of which seemed to have ample headroom.

After careful consideration to the fallen tree debris on the roof, buckled sidewalk, direction of leaning, and variety of bugs that lived in the tree, Mom decided it had to go. She contacted the city and sometime later a crew showed up to remove it. The workers climbed the tree carefully removing and lowering the branches to the ground. A two-man chain saw was used to dismantle the trunk and slice it into moveable pieces. One man even wielded a large double-bladed axe nipping off many small branches. This four-year-old boy stood on the side porch and witnessed the whole process as it unfolded. As for the remaining stump, that was to be dealt with at a much later time.

Much additional work needed to be done that first summer. A large trash pile at the end of the driveway had been left by the previous occupants. This needed to be gathered and carted to the dump. The back quarter of the yard needed to be hand tilled for a small vegetable garden. All the house windows needed to be washed, freed up, and caulked. The front porch was sagging and the supports were replaced with a cement block wall the full length of the front. Along with all these tasks other items needed attention, like a furnace and chimney cleaning, heater duct and cold air return cleaning, along with a complete cellar and attic cleaning. Coal bins needed repair and canned goods storage shelving built.

Somehow the work managed to get done and the bungalow on Steuben Street became our warm and cozy home.

MY FAMILY

~

My father was a tall, slender, and hardworking man. He was born n Clinton, New York in the year 1912, the son of Robert Francis Overend and Ellen Frances Overend (nee: Greenfield). Dad had three younger brothers: Thomas, Joseph, and Robert (Joseph's twin who died in infancy).

Dad always walked with a slight limp. This was the result of a childhood incident when he accidentally dumped a small kettle of boiling water down his right leg. During the healing process his small toe attached itself to the adjacent toe in an awkward position. He carved two small slits into all his right shoes in order to relieve the soreness from the pressure.

When I was born in the year 1942 World War II was raging overseas. Like many young men at that time Dad received notification that he was being drafted into the Army. I was two weeks old when he took his induction physical and passed it with flying colors, injured foot and all. He was scheduled to leave immediately for boot camp so he gave his notice that Friday at work.

Dad was employed at a small company on Court Street in Syracuse named Cine Simplex Corp. as a tool and die maker. When he turned in his notice Cine Simplex contacted the Army and insisted that Dad not be drafted. For reasons unknown to my family at that time my father was issued a deferment and assigned to a United States Coast Guard unit in the Port of Oswego as a machinist (boat operator). He continued working at Cine Simplex and was exempt from military deployment.

His work at Cine Simplex continued well beyond the time we moved into our Steuben Street home. He was well into his sixties age wise before we found out that Dad was making precision parts for the highly classified Norden bombsights. These bombsights were mechanical computers that interfaced with aircraft autopilot systems to provide very accurate bomb drops over enemy targets including one of the first atomic bombs.

My mother Helen and her twin sister Anne were born in the year 1913 in a white farm house near Corkins Lane in Galeville, New York. Her parents were Joseph and Michaelina Bugnacki (nee: Gadomska). Mom was a very regimented individual and ruled with an iron-willed personality. In other words, my sister and I had to be prepared to go up against the ocean tide if we were caught venturing beyond the limits of her authority.

Mom was also a hard worker. She had to leave school at the end of her fifth grade year to stay home and help raise her brother Frank since her mother needed to tend the counter in the Galeville store. In addition, Mom would also work in the store when needed.

My mother worked in several places during her youth. When she was fifteen years old she lied about her age and secured a position with Syracuse China located on Court Street in Syracuse, New York. Her job consisted of using a metal blade to remove rough edges from dining plates before they were fired in the furnace. Mom also worked at the Hill Top Laundry on Pond Street in Syracuse pressing sheets in a large steam press. The one job I think she liked the best in her younger years was at the Paul DeLima coffee plant in downtown Syracuse tying string vertically around bags of ground coffee that were to be delivered to grocery stores. Just think, this was an era before twisty ties were invented.

My father and mother were married at Sacred Heart Church on the Fourth of July in the year 1935. The Great Depression that ravaged throughout the United States was in full swing. Their total income at that time was $9.36 a week.

In the early years of their marriage Mom and Dad had rented apartments around the north side of Syracuse where Dad had grown up. They were living upstairs in a two family house in the 1200 block of Park Street when I was born in 1942. When my sister Elaine was born in 1943 they were renting an apartment in the 900 block of Wadsworth Street. In November of 1943 they had managed to save enough money to purchase a lot with a garage on Hopkins Road in nearby Liverpool. Dad worked very hard building us a small home where we lived until February 1946 when we moved to Steuben Street in Syracuse.

THE OCTOPUS

In the 1940s many urban bungalows had a octopus in the basement. The octopus was a gravity furnace that provided heat throughout the home during the winter seasons.

Our octopus took up significant space in the basement. The body of the furnace was about four feet in diameter and stood as a large cylinder with a somewhat rounded dome. Round ductwork existed in all directions from the top of the furnace body. These ducts carried the heated air to grilled openings called registers located in each of the main floor rooms. Additional ductwork provided air returns for several locations throughout the main floor to the base of the furnace. The grills for these were known as cold air boxes and provided the pathway for cooler room air to be recycled and reheated.

The octopus had no electric motors or thermostats to simplify operation. Inside the outer cylindrical body was a chamber known as the firebox. The firebox had grates installed about two feet above the bottom so that ashes from the fire could drop to the bottom for removal. A large lever on the outside of the furnace provided the means to shake the grates back- and-forth to drop ashes as appropriate.

Since thermostats were not yet available for furnaces, a simpler but effective control was used. Sash chain was attached to small door openings in the main doors of the furnace. These chains ran vertical and up through holes in the floor to a metal box mounted on an adjacent upstairs wall. These chains would allow the small doors to be opened and closed in small increments thereby letting more or less air to enter the firebox. This would control the intensity of the fuel burn and ultimately the temperature throughout the living areas.

Generally, the octopus was not started until the winter weather and colder outdoor temperatures warranted it. As I indicated previously, there are no thermostats, electric motors, or electronic attachments. Starting and running the octopus was tedious and required periodic monitoring. This was a job that fell in the scope of father's responsibility.

Coal was probably the most popular fuel burned in the octopus. Unfortunately, getting coal to burn is a multistep process. There are two types of coal used back in the 1940s, anthracite and bituminous. Anthracite is a hard coal that burns hotter and longer. It was preferred for use in the octopus. Bituminous is a softer coal customarily used in kitchen or parlor stoves.

The control chains located on the main living area are pulled and set to allow the draft plates to be slightly open on the firebox doors. Kindling wood is stacked in the fire box and a small wood fire is started. Once the wood fire has produced hot embers, a couple of shovels of bituminous coal is added and allowed to burn. Only then will the fire be hot enough to ignite the anthracite coal. Three or four shovels of anthracite are inserted into the firebox and banked against itself for a long progressive burn.

To keep the fire burning continuously the octopus needs tending every few hours. In most instances the grates need shaking to remove ash from the underside of the burning coal to allow for a good air intake. Also, the ashes and cinders must be removed from the base of the firebox and stored in metal tubs called ash cans to cool for disposal.

This old octopus kept the long winter nights on Steuben Street warm and cozy.

DOG DAYS

During the late 1940s and early 1950s the hottest and most-humid days of summer arrived on schedule in last weeks of July and first weeks of August. This particular time period was named the Dog Days of Summer. We children were encouraged to control our physical activities and avoid overexertion. We wiled away our hottest days sitting on the front porch steps playing cards, board games, and paddle ball. An occasional walk was taken to the corner store for a five-cent ice-cream bar.

As with much of the North side, Steuben Street was lined with mostly elm, ash, and chestnut trees. They provided a shady midday canopy from the hot sun. There were no home air-conditioners. The only indoor cooling were warm breezes that blew through window or porch door screens. It seemed that on the hottest days there was no breeze at all.

The Dog Days of the 1940s and '50s also ushered in a more foreboding annual event - a ravaging viral disease known as poliomyelitis, or more simply - polio. One of the sounds-of-summer that brought a stir to our emotions was the wail of an ambulance siren. In many instances it meant only one thing - another child or young adult being rushed to the hospital with the dreaded polio symptoms.

The source of the Polio virus was unknown, although the common housefly was suspected to be a major carrier. Many children that contacted this disease ended up paralyzed from the waist down needing crutches and leg braces in order to walk again. There were an unfortunate number of victims that were paralyzed from the chest down. In order to continue breathing they had to be placed into a large respirator called an iron lung.

An iron lung was a long cylindrical chamber made of metal and mounted horizontally on a metal frame. The convalescing individual was placed on their back inside the chamber with only their head outside. The pressure within the chamber was cycled continuously, thereby providing an artificial means of operating the individual's lungs.

The iron lung was operated twenty-four hours a day by an electric motor. Should the motor fail, a lever was provided for manual operation. A sign stating IRON LUNG was attached to the front of every home containing such a device. If a power failure occurred in the neighborhood, residents nearby would rush to these homes and take turns pumping the iron lung until electricity was restored.

I remember one such sign was displayed on the front porch rail of a home around the corner on Park Street. I did not learn until a couple of years later that the stricken boy within was the brother of my classmate. He was fortunate enough to be able to return to school with leg braces and on crutches. Back then people tended to be very private and kept their misfortunes quietly to themselves.

Since the cause and cure were unknown, strict parental rules were generated and enforced during the Dog Days of summer. All porch doors were opened and closed quickly to keep as many flies out as possible. Sticky flypaper was hung in at least two rooms of the home to catch the intruders. We were forbid to visit the local swimming pools. No drinks were to be swapped or shared. Proper hand washing was essential. In 1955 the major breakthrough that everyone had hoped and prayed for actually happened. A doctor named Jonas Salk introduced us to the polio vaccine he had developed. Supplies of the vaccine went into distribution to doctors throughout the country. My mother immediately scheduled my sister and me for our first shot of the three-shot vaccination series. She took us downtown to Dr. Reidell's office on West Onondaga Street for the initial shot. A month later we took the bus ourselves for the second round. And, a few months later we had the final shot.

The families that lived on Steuben Street were truly blessed. I don't recall ever seeing an IRON LUNG sign posted on a Steuben Street home.

Dog Day freedom at last - maybe. The Dog Day restrictions were slow to go away. The original precautions remained in place for several years afterward. The Salk vaccine proved itself to be a success. Eventually the hottest, most-humid days of summer reigned over tragedies of the polio season.

COAL MAN

The furnace and stoves in our Steuben Street home all used coal to provide heating during the winter months. Three-sided wooden bins were constructed along the cellar walls to house the coal - one for hard and another for soft coal. Each bin was located directly beneath a cellar window that provided access for coal delivery. Like most commodities, coal was less expensive off-season so summer delivery fit the budget. It was a big event the day Mom would announce that the Coal Man would be coming to deliver the coal. This was big news. Coal delivery was an annual event that could not be missed by young ones.

The coal was delivered in dump trucks. The back of the dump truck was partitioned into three sections. Each section held a ton of coal. Once the rearmost section was emptied the driver could release the next partition and free the next section of coal for delivery. Our hard and soft coal were delivered in the same truck, each in a separate section.

The Coal Man was the driver of the truck. He was always donned in overalls, a billed cap, and clouded completely in black soot. Like most, our driveway was very narrow. The Coal Man's initial task was to back the truck into the driveway and position the rear within a few feet of the cellar window. Once the cellar window was removed a chute wad connected below the small door located at the rear of the dump truck box. An additional chute was attached to channel the coal through the cellar window directly into the coal bin. The coal chutes were rectangular and closely resembled a playground slide. Then, the event we kids all waited for commenced.

The Coal Man pulled on the long handle raising the dump box door. The coal would rush out and down the chute with a loud roar that could be heard several houses away. This was summer magic. When the roar started to diminish the Coal Man would keep raising the dump box until each section had emptied. The thrill was leaning over the back porch rail, fingers in ears, and watching every piece of coal ride down that chute.

The show did not end there. The Coal Man would reposition his truck at the next cellar window and fill the second coal bin. Once finished he would lower the dump box, stow the slides, collect the cash payment, hand write a receipt, and head for the next delivery location.

Something about the loud roar mesmerized us over and over again each summer. It was one of those childhood events that had to be watched each and every time no matter what.

Deliveries to homes that did not have driveways took on a different twist. The coal truck would park in the street at the curb and offload into wheelbarrows. The wheelbarrows were then dumped one by one into the coal bin. A small chute extended into the cellar window. Although we did not consider this to be an extravagant event, it was well worth spending time watching.

THE HING

The coldest months of Winter occurred in January and February. The octopus furnace provided sufficient heating for the majority of the rooms in our home. The kitchen and back room always seemed to require some additional warmth. This warmth was obtained from the firebox in the kitchen stove.

Choosing the fuel used depended primarily upon what the outside temperature was. During somewhat warmer days my mother would use scrap wood pieces and start a fire just long enough to take the chill out of the room. During the coldest part of winter my father would remove the firebox grates and install a kerosene pot-burner inside the firebox compartment. A small kerosene tank stood vertically on a perch directly behind the stove and metered fuel to the burner. This burner ran continuously and the can could be removed periodically, refilled, and placed back into position without interrupting the burner operation.

From about the age of seven, two of my chores consisted of splitting the scrap wood to proper stove size using a hatchet. That was always fun since it was done outside in nice fall weather. Keeping the kerosene tank filled was also a chore I inherited. This required me to lift the tank off the stand behind, invert it, and carefully remove the cap without damaging the pin valve that protruded from the cap. I would then need to carry the can down cellar and fill it from a larger barrel of kerosene located near the base of the cellar staircase, heft it back upstairs, reinstall the cap, and very carefully reposition it onto the stand without damaging the pin valve. This litany took place twice a day for as long as it was needed.

During the earlier and latter winter days we had a third option - coal. When using coal, the firebox would have grates installed at the base of the box itself. The grates were accessed via a small door on the front of the stove. A small crank handle sat beside the stove. When the door was opened the crank was slid onto the end of the grates. If coal was being added above, shaking the grates was necessary to allow burned coal ash to fall within the compartment below. Once cooled, these ashes would be removed with a small shovel and carted away in a metal ash can for disposal at a later time. This was yet another task that I was assigned along with fetching the coal when needed.

Needless to say, coal was needed quite often. My sister and I shared this task of trekking to the coal bin in the cellar several times each day. She was more astute at finding ways around this task than I was. Either way, fetching the coal became the most eerie chore of all, especially during the dark hours.

The trip to the coal bin started by carrying the empty coal pail through the poorly lit back room to the cellar door located at the farthest corner. The light switch for the cellar light was beside this door. Once the switch was thrown and the cellar door opened the stairway arrangement blocked much of the light from the one and only light bulb at that end of the cellar.

The stairway consisted of four or five steps down to a intermediate landing, then four or five more steps to the cellar floor. The coal bin was diagonally across the cellar floor at the bottom of the stairway. Unfortunately, the overhead light bulb was dim and it's light was significantly blocked from reaching the coal bin. Other areas of the cellar remained in total darkness.

Each time I approached the coal bin my hearing was acute and vision sharp. The area immediate to the bottom of the cellar stairway was dimly lit. Being located across the basement, the coal bin area was much more opaque and shadowy. A short distance left of the coal bin stood the octopus ever guarding the area of nocturnal darkness.

Although the basement was safe, my sister and I always felt there was an unknown presence lurking in the dingy pitch-black abyss at night. We were both fully convinced that this unknown invisible phantom actually existed. Every little sound or noise reinforced our ghostly belief that there truly was a Hing in our presence.

To us this Hing was the keeper of the darkness. This was his abode and he would always be skulking about looking for intruders, especially young children. The perception we shared was one of never leaving the protection of a lit area sine the Hing only lurked in total darkness.

Hauling buckets of coal at night for the kitchen became a tenuous task. To make matters worse, my sister and I would play pranks on each other at the expense of the Hing. We became so obsessed with the Hing that we both feared the dreaded trip to the coal bin. Initially, we fervently lied as to whose turn it was to fetch the coal. It got elevated to the point where my mother would intercede and order one of us to go down immediately. Of course, the unassigned sibling would smile, giggle, and always whisper a reminder about the Hing being down there. The ultimate prank was soon to evolve. What superb idea could one devise to spook the other with?

The perfect scheme involved sneaking across the back room to the cellar door, listening for the sound of coal being shoveled into the pail, then turning off the one-and-only cellar light while yelling the word "Hing" a couple of times. This required great skill because a rapid retreat was absolutely necessary in order to avoid the parental consequences when the screams of bloody murder erupted downstairs. Although successfully executed, these missions almost always resulted in disciplinary action on the part of our mother. She absolutely hated us kids screaming.

Although a true apparition never materialized, the Hing was with us a very long time. Even in her old age my mother would always ask us if we remembered the Hing. She always wondered where we got the name "Hing" from. We could never satisfy her curiosity because we did not know. It was just a silly name we thought up in a childhood moment.

If you are ever in a dark basement be careful, the Hing may be watching your every move.

THE UBIQUITOUS BOX

In the fall of 1948 I was just starting in the Second Grade. My sister was in First Grade. for full-day classes. I can only imagine, my mother must have been ecstatic.

World War II was now behind us and people were once again healing from the tragedies of war. Radios were abundant and proved to be a never-ending source of both news and entertainment.

We had two radios in our home. One was a console radio that tuned in local radio stations and short-wave ones as well. This radio sat in our parlor and was used on special occasions only. Our second radio was a small table radio the sat on a wall shelf in our kitchen. My mother used it for daily news and weather reports. Some evenings after supper my father would carefully lift it from the shelf and place it on the kitchen table. He would enjoy listening to fifteen-minute shows like "The Lone Ranger" and newscasts with Walter Winchell. The highlight of the week was the lively polka music every Sunday morning at 11:00 AM on the "Polish Serenade" program.

Although radios had been around for awhile and were obviously here to stay, signs were beginning to be painted on the sides of brick buildings announcing a new phenomenon called television. Although tested in other parts of the United States, the first television transmitting station in Syracuse would not become operational until late in 1948. Naturally, observing the beginnings of this wonder firsthand was the experience of a lifetime for this six year old. It was a curiosity of a lifetime.

In December of 1948 the first television broadcast station was touted as coming to life. A million questions filled my brain. How do people travel through radio waves? How come I can't see them? When do they sleep? Where do they live? This station was called Channel 8. What is a Channel 8? How come it's not on the radio? The station is only eight blocks or less from my house. How come I can't see anything?

Springtime came in 1949 and I was no closer to finding out what television was. My father took my sister and me with him to a hardware store named "Dotter and Becker's" located on North Salina Street not too far from Assumption Church. Upon leaving the store we noticed people gathered across the street peering into a storefront window. Dad then took us across the street and to our surprise there was a television set staring out at us through the store window. The picture area was round and about six inches in diameter. The color was called black- and-white but to me it was light-gray-and-dark-gray. The picture was fuzzy and did not seem to be very well focused. I left there not realizing that this mysterious box was intended for anyone's living room should they desired to purchase it.

Time continued moving on. One evening we walked over to our Uncle Johnny and Aunt Marie Greenfield's house on Park Street. When we sat down in their parlor we could not help but notice a large sculpted cabinet standing nestled across the room. Although we were taught never to snoop or ask impolite questions our curiosity began to run wild. Finally, we had to ask just what this was. My Aunt Marie turned to Uncle Johnny and told him to open the two doors and show us the television set. The picture area on this set was about ten inches in diameter. He turned it on and it began making a low humming sound. After a minute or so the picture screen began to glow and Uncle Johnny began tuning it to the local transmitting station.

Suddenly, a picture appeared along with accompanying sound. My sister and I were viewing a puppet show titled "Lucky Pup" and loved every minute of it. The show ended about five minutes later and the television was turned off.

Somehow we found out that "Lucky Pup" was on every Thursday evening at 7:00 PM for approximately fifteen minutes. We drove our parents crazy with endless pleas to visit Aunt Marie and Uncle Johnny at this time weekly. Discipline ruled and we were not allowed to impose on relatives just to watch a television program.

Life moved on as it always had and television seemed to be just a novelty. A second television station had arrived in Syracuse shortly after the first began operation. Some of our school classmates would occasionally mention a television show or two. We had more important things like homework to complete, handball games to play, marbles to win, chestnuts to collect, and many other events to occupy our time with.

By Fall 1951 I was well on my way through fourth-grade. School would dismiss about 2:30 in the afternoon. My sister and I would walk the two blocks home together on a regular basis. Upon arriving home one warm afternoon we dropped our books on the kitchen table as usual. Then, scurrying through the sitting room to change out of our school clothes we notice something rather large on the table covered completely over with a blanket. My mother wanted us to wait until our father was there for the unveiling.

Our curiosity abounded. We could not peek under the blanket and had absolutely no idea what this was. A very small portion of one corner protruded a bit and indicated perhaps a wooden box of sorts. The size and shape resembled a three-foot cubed shape. We then got down to doing homework. Nothing in our home ever took place until homework was completed each day.

Dad worked in a machine shop evenings and would not be home until Midnight. Of course we would be in bed and asleep long before that time. Any hope of seeing what was under the blanket would have to wait until the next day. Sneaking a peek was out of the question. Parental disobedience was never tolerated. Sneaking would be considered a breach in trust and whatever this was would be returned to the store as a punishment. Values meant everything when we were growing up.

We raced home from school the next day. Dad was there and after some coaxing we all gathered by the object and the blanket was removed. Perched there inside our home was none other than a brand new television set. We were as excited and surprised as could be. Another day would lapse before seeing our television in operation, but that did not matter. We now had a television and that was that.

It was early afternoon the next day when we gathered to see our new FADA television operate for the first time. Dad plugged the power cord into a wall outlet and turned the power switch on. After approximately one minute the picture screen glowed with a gray-white glow. Then the struggle began.

Eight knobs were located on the front side of the TV across the bottom area. The right-hand knobs were nested within each other and were used for tuning into a broadcast station. The largest knob was rotated in either direction until an image appeared on the screen. The smaller knob would then be used to make fine adjustments to the tuner for capturing the best signal reception.

Once a station was acquired, the remaining six knobs were used to adjust the picture quality for viewing. The television set operated with a large quantity of vacuum tubes within. The vacuum tubes had filaments that glowed and heated the tube for operation. A lot of heat accumulated within the television box and this would cause the electronic circuitry to slowly drift when viewing the picture. Because of this several adjustments had to be made periodically while the set was in operation.

For example, manually adjusting the Fine tuning knob would keep the set tuned to the optimum signal being received for the specific channel being watched. The Contrast and Brightness knobs were used to establish the best picture quality for the program being watched. Periodically the internal heat would alter the performance of the electronic parts within the set and the picture would tend to roll vertically or horizontally on the screen. The Vertical and Horizontal knobs were then adjusted to stop these undesired and unwanted motions. This ritual continued each and every time the television was in operation.

Once shut off the television set would cool down. When turned on the next day, the ritual would restart all over again.

The very first show we watched on our new television was a local program on cooking with a lady named Kay Larson. Programs would air for fifteen-minute intervals with sometimes hours before another would appear. During the off time the station would generate a test pattern that looked like a target. It contained circles, multi-sized bar patterns, and various gray shades. This pattern was used so the individual television set could be adjusted properly for size and shape. Although this was somewhat helpful, it did not resolve the ritual of set readjustment when powered up after resting.

As time went on, more and more shows started to appear. Although exciting to watch, television was far from becoming an obsession. It always took a back seat to school, homework, chores, music lessons, and outdoor activities.

THE GALEVILLE STORE

The Galeville Store was a small grocery store located on Old Liverpool Road about halfway between the Syracuse north side boundary and the Village of Liverpool. In the mid 1940s it was still very much a quaint rural setting.

Excitement abounded each time my sister and I climbed into the back seat of Dad's 1936 Chevy to head out and visit the store. Since the store was owned and operated by our maternal grandparents Joseph and Lena Bugnacki, we always felt like we were in for a good time. Grandpa and Grandma Bugnacki sold basic staples that included cold-cuts, assorted canned goods, bread, soap, and, best of all, penny candy.

Riding to the Galeville Store consisted of a very short side step form Steuben Street to Park Street, then North on Park Street until it merged with the Old Liverpool Road. The trip took us past our school and church (St. John the Baptist Parish), around a small park with a horse-watering fountain called Washington Square, over several railroad tracks where, on occasion, we would get to see a big steam locomotive in action, by the Regional Farmers Market, and directly to the store.

Upon arriving at the store we would enter a large dirt driveway and park behind the store itself. The store was situated approximately in the center of Galeville. With the exception of a few houses on either side and several directly across the road, much of the surrounding land was undeveloped. The building itself was a two-story structure. The store was located downstairs while Grandpa and Grandma's living quarters were upstairs. Upon entering the back door, the store entry was straight ahead and two steps down. The stairway to the upstairs living quarters was directly left inside this entry.

Grandpa and Grandma did not have indoor plumbing during the early 1940s. As a result, outside the back door about fifty feet away stood the outhouse. I learned at a very young age that anything and everything said describing an out house was definitely true.

Some distance further back from the outhouse stood a line of low profile sheds called salt covers. Although no longer used at that time, they originally housed large flat wood trays. Salt mined from nearby springs was spread in these trays for drying. The roof of each shed was capable of sliding on rails to expose the salt for drying on fair-weather days.

A cast bronze farm bell was mounted on the peak of the Galeville Store roof. A rope attached to the bell crank hung two-stories down on the side of the store and was tethered to a location on the small side porch. Whenever it would begin to rain the bell would be rung and neighbors would rush to pull the covers back over the exposed salt to prevent it from getting wet.

Across the front of the Galeville Store was a covered wooden walkway. The store entrance consisted of double-doors located directly in the center. Once inside, wooden shelves on the right held canned goods, dry cereal, oatmeal, and soap. On the left was the counter with the meat cooler nested next inline. Among other things the counter held a large roll of brown paper for wrapping meats, pickles, etc. A coffee bean grinder and several glass jars of penny candy also occupied space on the counter.

Being curious, I was always attracted to the medium-size vinegar barrel that sat sideways on a stand near the back door. It had a spigot and tap on one end to allow for filling customer orders. Invariably, Grandpa Bugnacki kept a sharp eye on me since I could never seem to overcome the temptation of opening the tap and getting vinegar on the floor.

Grandma Bugnacki always greeted us with a big smile and a hug. She was very kind to all her grandchildren. Although thoroughly warned by Mom in advance not to ask for candy, Grandma Bugnacki always handed us a small marshmallow candy cone. When Mom put her foot down about my sister and I eating candy Grandma would give us slices of ring bologna instead.

Grandma and Grandpa Bugnacki were immigrants that emigrated to America in order to escape the harshness they experienced in Poland. Grandma Bugnacki (nee Michaelina Gadomska) was born in Ligowo Plock, Poland in 1888. Grandma arrived in America in 1898 at the age of nine with her mother Balbina, sister Julianna, and brother Stanley. They established residence in Syracuse and eventually had a small farm in the Town of Salina near Liverpool, New York.

Grandpa Bugnacki was born in Lomza, Poland in 1874. Grandpa came to America in 1903 with only ten dollars in his pocket. Grandpa had three brothers, Peter, Iggots, and Stanley, who also emigrated to America. They settled in Syracuse, New York.

Grandpa and Grandma Bugnacki were married in 1904 at the Sacred Heart Church on West Genesee Street in Syracuse, New York. Through the years they had twelve children including four sets of twins. My mother Helen was one of the twins.

As the Bugnacki family grew, ample space was needed to house the family. Living quarters above the Galeville Store became available for rent so the family moved to Galeville. Grandpa worked in the grocery store and eventually arranged to purchase it.

Although Grandma Bugnacki had little trouble learning the English language, Grandpa found it to be a struggle. Persevering through it all, they both managed to obtain American citizenship by 1939. The Syracuse newspaper even wrote and published a nice article on Grandpa's accomplishment.

As with all our visits to Grandma and Grandpa's store, eventually it was time to return home to Steuben Street. On the way back our mother would run through the litany of all the things we should and should not have done. Subsequent visits proved that we must not have been too bad. Grandma always had that beautiful smile as she stood behind the candy jars and Grandpa just went about his business while keeping an ever vigilant eye on me and the vinegar barrel.

KINDERGARTEN

A short while after we moved into our Steuben Street bungalow my mother told me that I would be starting school soon. Early that summer in 1946 she had enrolled me at St. John the Baptist Academy (a Roman Catholic school) nearby on Park Street. My sister was due for a vaccination that was held at a public school in the same locale. My mother took me along and showed me what a school looked like and explained that the school I was to attend would look similar. I was fascinated and really looked forward to the day when I would start Kindergarten.

During the Spring months of 1946 I had experienced some difficulty with bouts of soar throat and swallowing. After a visit to the doctor it was decided that I would need to have my tonsils and adenoids removed. Because of my hoarseness Mom best described it as having a frog removed from my throat. The thought of it did not bother me a bit because I assumed this was a necessary prerequisite for getting into school.

When the day for surgery arrived, Dad and Mom piled me into the rear seat of our 1936 Chevy coupe and headed downtown to the

Medical Arts Building where the operation would take place. Mom prepared me by mentioning that I would put on my pajamas, lay down on a table, and have a small ether can placed over my nose so I would fall asleep.

Upon arriving at the Medical Arts Building on East Genesee Street in Syracuse everything began as Mom had predicted. I put my pajamas on and settled nicely onto the operating room table. There was a bright light overhead and the nurse placed a somewhat translucent cloth over my eyes. The doctor was there as someone positioned the small container of ether anesthetic over my nose. The doctor told me to count up starting at one. The next thing I remember was waking up.

I was in a small dark room. The window was covered with a closed venetian blind. A nurse was seated at the foot of my bed in the corner of the room. As I stirred, she walked over to tell me that my mother had left for awhile but would return shortly. My throat was sore so I asked for a glass of water. The nurse drew me a drink of warm water. When I asked her for ice water she told me I would have to wait a couple of days for that. I then fell back to sleep.

The next time I awoke the blinds were partially open and the room was sunny and bright. Mom and Dad were there to take me home. Leaving my pajamas on, Dad wrapped me in an army blanket that he brought along and carried me down the street to our car.

Although sore initially, the pain dissipated significantly over a short period of time. A diet that included small amounts of vanilla ice cream certainly helped the recovery. Before long the pain and hoarseness was totally gone. Now I felt qualified to take the big step and start school.

September of 1946 had finally arrived. On the first Wednesday after Labor Day my Mom helped me dress for my very first day at school. We walked out the side porch door and it was a nice sunny day. Mom walked me down Steuben Street to Kirkpatrick Street, turned right and continued a short distance to Park Street. Turning left onto Park Street, we walked another block to Danforth Street and arrived at the school. All along the way Mom pointed out landmarks and street corners so I could begin to absorb the route. She made sure that I knew she would be with me each day until I was sure of finding my own way alone.

St. John the Baptist Academy consisted of two separate two-story brick buildings joined by an elevated passageway on the top floor of each building. The front building had classrooms for students in grade four through grade twelve. The smaller building was for grades three and below.

Directly on the corner of Danforth and Park Streets sat a large red house. This was the convent where the Sisters of Saint Joseph resided. The Sisters were the school teachers for all grade levels. Mom showed me where to enter a large play yard in back of the larger school building. We both crossed the yard and approached a pair of heavy wooden doors on the side of the small building. Upon entering we turned immediately to the room on the right and the door was open. This was my Kindergarten classroom.

The first person I met was my teacher, Sister Elizabeth Charles. Mom told me that I would stay there for class and she would be back to meet me outside when class was dismissed for the day. Sister Elizabeth Charles took me over to a large metal sandbox that sat on the far side of the room beneath the windows. One other boy was there at the time and we shared some toy cars while making roads in the sand.

It was not long before other children arrived and the class came to order. We were assigned our very own small chairs that were lined up in a double row facing the head of the classroom. A few of the other children began to cry for a little while. I did not understand that because I thought school was great. Sure enough, the first day ended and there was Mom standing at the door as I left.

I arrived at school on time everyday and Mom was always there at Noon like clockwork. One day Mom walked behind and let me lead the way to and from. The next day she told me I would make the walk alone. On the way to school I kept looking back but Mom was nowhere to be seen. When school let out I carefully crossed at Danforth Street, walked up Park Street, and there on the corner at Kirkpatrick Street stood Mom. Although I knew the way well by then, she just had to make sure. After that trip I was totally on my own for real.

We did a lot of exciting things in Kindergarten like learning the alphabet, coloring pictures, memorizing words, counting numbers, cutting, pasting, and grasping how to read. We each had a book of our very own titled "Dick and Jane" that we read from often. On occasion we would each have a percussion type musical instrument and learn how to keep time to music. Sister Elizabeth had a record player and march music. My musical instrument consisted of two cylindrical shaped hardwood sticks about nine inches long that would be struck together to the tempo of the song being played. Other children had small cymbals, tambourines, or drums. I don't recall one music class where everyone was in synchronization. We had chocolate milk breaks, quiet time, and play time outside in good weather. During the school year we had time off for Thanksgiving and Christmas as well as national holidays that occurred throughout the year.

Spring was well on its way and our class was preparing for the celebration of Easter Sunday. Being a Catholic school, we were taught Christian aspects of all the holidays and holy days. We learned the meaning of thankfulness at Thanksgiving, the joy in the birth of the Christ child at Christmas, and the supreme sacrifice Christ made for the salvation of all mankind that became known as Easter.

Our class was dismissed from school on the Wednesday before Easter and we were not scheduled to return until the following Monday. The following two days, Holy Thursday and Good Friday, commemorated the passion and crucifixion of Christ so us children were expected to attend church services as appropriate with our parents. Instead, Mom took my sister and me with her to care for someone very dear to her.

It was midday when we arrived at the Galeville store. We went quietly up the back stairway to Grandma and Grandpa Bugnacki's home. Grandpa was 73 years old and was bedridden with pneumonia. Mom helped to wash him, comb his hair, and feed him some broth she had prepared.

I remember entering the bedroom to say hello to him. Grandpa was hard of hearing so he did not hear me initially. Upon Mom's urging I reentered the room and bid my Grandpa a very loud greeting. He turned his head and acknowledged my greeting with a low and garbled response. It scared me, so I left the room and told my Mom. She then sat me down and told me that Grandpa was very ill but he did appreciate me talking to him.

Grandma was tending the store. I spent the day upstairs with my Mom and Grandpa. It was not a proper time to scurry through the store looking for candy treats. Later in the day Grandpa's care was turned over to one of my aunts and Dad drove us back home.

Saturday had arrived and my sister and I were feeling the anticipation of Easter Sunday. At church, the statues covered with purple cloth for the past forty days of the Lenten season would again be unveiled for viewing. In addition, the altars would all be adorned with white lilies, tulips, and lilacs in celebration of a Mass honoring the resurrection of Christ from the dead.

Although it was Holy Saturday, we could not help but ponder the mysterious arrival of an Easter Bunny that very night. Then, the telephone rang. Mom answered the phone, talked only for a short while, then hung up and began crying. One of Mom's sisters had called to let her know that Grandpa Bugnacki had passed away that very day.

Easter Sunday came and went. Mom spent time with her siblings and Grandma Bugnacki planning Grandpa's funeral. My sister and I were deemed too young to attend Grandpa's funeral. Grandpa's service was held at Sacred Heart Church on West Genesee Street.

Known affectionately as the "Polish Church" here in Syracuse, Grandpa had been an attendee since his arrival in America.

Even a Kindergarten boy was old enough to miss his Grandpa. Every Easter since then has been special to me. Among other things I will always remember the game of Cat-and-Mouse that Grandpa and I played at the vinegar barrel spigot.

It was only a week after Grandpa's funeral when my Dad, Mom, and sister celebrated my fifth Birthday. Mom always baked us a round cake from scratch and would ice it with a traditional hard sugar frosting.

Buds were popping and leaves were forming on the large trees that lined Steuben Street. The weather was warming quite nicely as the first day of May arrived. A shrine was erected outside in our school yard for a devotional service to the Blessed Virgin Mary. A statue of Mary was placed in the center of the handball court just outside our Kindergarten entrance. Vases of flowers decorated the area around the base of the statue. Our teachers gathered all the lower-grade students and positioned them about the school yard. After reciting a few basic prayers everyone would join in singing hymns. This was an exciting experience for our class that left me looking forward to learning how to sing.

Another prominent event was my sister's fourth birthday celebration occurring in mid-May. Again, our family of four gathered at the dinner table with homemade cake, icing, and candles.

It was not long before the month of June arrived. This meant that school was almost completed for this year. A graduation ceremony was being scheduled for later that June. My cousin Patty and

I traversed the same Kindergarten class together. Now we would graduate together.

Sister Elizabeth Charles handed me a paper to take home and give to my Mother. It was a piece that I needed to memorize and recite at the graduation ceremony. The wind was very brisk that particular day and the note was blown from my hand while walking up Park Street. Mom sent a note back to school and I managed to get another copy safely home the next day.

Graduation day arrived. We were all dressed in white caps and gowns. I gave my recitation without stumbling and it was well received. After the ceremony a photographer photographed my cousin Patty and me standing side-by-side. The photo was subsequently published under the title "Cousins Graduate" in one of the local newspapers.

Kindergarten was officially over. Summertime was here. The Fall of 1947 seemed so very far off at this particular moment. Play and fun were the only agenda for now.

A Childhood on Steuben Street

The author and his sister Elaine at play in the backyard of their Steuben Street home in 1948.

Elaine's Kindergarten graduation photo in 1948 alongside the Steuben Street home.

THE GREENFIELD'S

༄

The Greenfield Family lived in a large two-story house located in the 1200 block of Park Street. They were our relatives from my father's maternal side of the family and played a very important part in all our lives. To fully understand how this all fits together, the following history will help clarify the relationships.

Dad's paternal grandparents, Joseph and Mary Overend emigrated to America from Yorkshire, England in the year 1901 with their nine children. The settled in Clark Mills, New York where they were employed as weavers at the Hind and Harrison Plush Company. Dad's father, Robert Francis Overend, was the sixth child in the family.

Dad's mother, Ellen (Nellie) Frances Greenfield, was born in Clinton, New York. She had a brother John, sisters Elizabeth (Lizzie) and Ada. Ada died from a common childhood disease when she was a youngster.

Robert met, courted, and married Nellie in 1911. My father was their eldest son born in 1912. They resided in Clark Mills since my grandfather worked at the local textile mill. Three additional sons were born. One was a twin who died in infancy shortly after childbirth.

World War I was raging in Europe at that time. In addition, a massive influenza epidemic was sweeping America. My grandfather Robert was one of the unfortunate individuals that contacted influenza. His family tried their very best to nurse him back to health. On November 11, 1918 the great war ended. The armistice was signed and the troops were headed home. Unfortunately, on this very day of peace my grandfather passed away.

My father was only six years old and his brothers were younger. His mother Nellie was now alone raising the three boys. A year or so later she apparently made the decision to move from Clark Mills to Syracuse in hope of securing a job close to where her brother John and sister Lizzie lived.

Before leaving Clark Mills, grandma Nellie temporarily placed Dad and his brothers with a friend who had a farm in Westmoreland, New York. Although young, Dad was proud to pitch in and help around the farm. One of his favorite offerings was telling my sister and me how he would run out barefooted in the frost and look for a steamy cow plop to warm his feet in while rounding up cows for milking.

Although the farm proved to be a magical place for Dad, it was a different story for the farmer's wife. After a short time she announced that since she had no children of her own she was not about to raise someone else's.

One morning when Dad awoke she had him prepare his bag while she packed for the two younger boys. With haste she took them all to an orphanage in Utica, New York, dropped them there, and left. Dad never saw her again.

Meanwhile, his Aunt Lizzie Greenfield in Syracuse had gotten word and immediately took a trolly to the orphanage in Utica. When she arrived she was given the younger boys immediately. As for my father, he was not allowed to leave since he was in quarantine for thirty days. This kept him isolated from all the other children to prevent outbreaks of childhood diseases. It was a form of solitary confinement.

Luckily my Dad had his own trick up his sleeve. He stopped eating and drinking completely. After several days the orphanage relented and had Aunt Lizzie come back to take him home with her. When they came and told him Aunt Lizzie was on her way by trolley, he ate the biggest meal of his life.

Grandma Nellie eventually remarried and had two more children. Dad and his next oldest brother Tom continued to live with their Aunt Lizzie in Syracuse. Joseph, the youngest, lived with his mother, half-sister Mary, and half-brother Henry.

My father lived with his Aunt Lizzie Greenfield until he was twenty-three years old. He then moved out on his own and married Mom. Although she was my great aunt we always called her Aunt Lizzie. She was a tall lady with blonde hair, braided and wrapped up on top of her head. Aunt Lizzie worked as a secretary all her life and never married. We always enjoyed visiting with her and her large black cat named Winkey.

Aunt Lizzie's brother John owned the house on Park Street. He and his wife Marie lived in the upstairs half along with their son Robert. Aunt lizzie occupied the downstairs half.

The Greenfield home stood majestically in the middle of the block. The outside was covered with a yellow-brick stucco siding. A sidewalk ran from the front, down the side, and circled around the back corner of the house. The driveway consisted of two rows of paving brick that extended from the street on up to a three-car garage that sat behind the house. The areas between the garage and house as well as the sidewalk and driveway were adorned with beautiful flower gardens that were planted and meticulously maintained by Aunt Lizzie. The back yard had fruit trees and a large vegetable garden that was tended by Uncle Johnny.

One recollection I have from early childhood is visiting Uncle Johnny and Aunt Marie to play with their collie dog Lucky. Another more somber memory goes back to the year 1945 when I was three years old and my grandmother Nellie had passed away. Her coffin was laid out in Aunt Lizzie's parlor. To keep expenses to a manageable amount, it was the practice back then to hold calling hours in a private residence rather than a funeral home. Aunt Lizzie was always there to help whenever needed.

Another practice was to hang a black wreath on the front door of the home where a deceased relative's wake was being held. When we were in the vicinity of a house displaying a black wreath it was traditional to be very quiet so as not to disturb the mourners. We were encouraged to say a prayer for the family. If a family member was nearby we would offer our condolences and quietly leave.

Grandma Nellie lived nearby on Oak Street. Dad never talked much about his mother. She was very poor since her second husband spent most of his money at a local bar. As a young boy during the Depression Years, Dad would go down to the train yard with a pail to collect scraps of coal so his mother would have heat. One train fireman in particular would shout for him to leave. As Dad looked up this same fireman would smile as he kicked some coal off the tender for Dad to fill his bucket. Dad would also walk around the neighborhood streets looking for scraps of wood for his mother to burn.

The Greenfield's were Dad's closest family in Syracuse and since we lived only a block away we were able to visit together quite often throughout the years.

It was not uncommon to hold a wedding reception in someone's backyard during the 1940's. One such reception took place at the Greenfield home when son Robert married his sweetheart Teresa Calogero during the summer of 1947.

Although only a block away, Dad drove us over there that day. Since we arrived early so Mom and Dad could help set things up, our car was parked directly in front of the house. The three-car garage was emptied out and decorated with white crape paper. Tables lined the various sections of the garage. The wedding cake sat on a table in the back corner of the first garage stall directly under a white bridal tissue paper bell that rocked in the breeze.

We had a distant cousin named Alvin that was an accordion player. Alvin sat outside near the end of the sidewalk and provided all the music that day. I spent as much time as I could watching him and became totally fascinated with the accordion. I told my mother that I wanted to learn how to play accordion music. Her immediate advice was to wait until I was a little older to be sure that I was truly interested.

By the time the reception had ended it was dark outside. Since Alvin lived across the city, Dad had offered to drive him home. We all piled into our 1936 chevy. Dad turned on to Spencer Street only to discover that the right rear tire had gone flat. He pulled up under a street light and we all stood beside the car while the tire was changed.

Once back on the road my sister and I slept until after Alvin was dropped off and we had arrived back home. The reception was over and within a few days Uncle Johnny had his garage back to normal. One thing though, the white bridal tissue paper bell still hung in the corner and continued to do so many years later.

FIRST GRADE

With the Summer of 1947 winding down, school was to begin once again. I was now starting First Grade and was actually looking forward to a full day session rather than the half-day sessions I was accustomed to in Kindergarten. My sister would be starting Kindergarten so Mom would get a much needed break at least for a half-day anyway.

The First Grade classroom entry was directly across from the Kindergarten room. Although Mom walked to school with both or us for the first few days, it eventually became my responsibility to escort my sister to class in the mornings and back home at lunchtime.

Living only a block or so from the school allowed us to have lunch at home each day.

My First Grade teacher was Sister Betilda Joseph. She was a very gentle and kind person. She treated us children with dignity and we all respected her. The classroom was quiet and very well organized. The desks had ornate metal sides that were anchored directly into the hardwood floor. The desk tops were wood with a small compartment directly under the writing surface where we stored our books, paper, crayons, and pencils. The seat was attached directly to the next desk behind and folded down for seating and up for easy cleaning when class ended.

The back of the room was lined with closets containing hangers and shelves for storage of our outdoor clothing such as coats, boots, hats, etc. Metal pane windows lined the left side of the classroom and could be opened on both the bottom and top for ventilation. Directly under the windows sat large silver-colored radiators that provided steam heat during the winter months. The front and right side walls were lined with large slate blackboards that included wood rails for holding chalk and erasers. Sister Betilda's desk resided up front in the center of the room facing the array of student desks.

A narrow row of cork boards stretched full length above all the blackboards. As the school year progressed we found out that the cork board was used to display our individual class work accomplishments.

A crucifix hung centered above the cork boards on the front wall. The American flag hung from a short flag pole mounted on the right side of the front wall. From the very first, we started each day reciting a prayer and then pledging allegiance to the flag.

Although the bank of windows provided a lot of daylight, artificial light was also needed. Six incandescent lights were suspended from the ceiling on the end of chains about four feet long. The lights were each covered by white frosted glass globes and arranged in a rectangular array consisting of two columns each with three rows directly above the student desks.

Our first subject every day was Religion. We were introduced to the Baltimore Catechism where we were taught the basics of the Catholic Church starting with the premise that God made us all in His image and likeness. From there we progressed to understanding the difference between good and bad. Proper behavior and respect were taught, accepted, and expected at all times.

Music became part of our classroom activity. Our music teacher would stop by once a week. She taught us simple basics of reading music, harmonizing to the tone of a pitch pipe, singing the musical scales, and singing songs as a group. The very first song our class learned to sing was the old standard titled "Gray Squirrel."

As the time passed the winter season was soon upon us again. This meant bundling up tightly for the walk to school each morning. Much as it was my responsibility to escort my sister safely to and from school, one cold wintery morning proved how shocking it was to witness an event that involved a loved one.

My sister and I left the house for school on time. A short while later we stood at the corner of Park and Kirkpatrick streets waiting to cross. For some unknown reason my sister lurched away from the rest of us and ran across the street. A car coming down the hill attempted to stop but could not quite manage. His front bumper hit my sister on the hip and flung her a short distance into a snow bank. She immediately got up and ran home.

Being somewhat in shock, I had no idea what to do. The driver asked who she was but I could not answer. Emotions whirled because we were taught not to talk with strangers and never go near a car that stopped. The driver left and I continued on to school.

When I arrived I told my first grade teacher that my sister had gone back home ill and probably would not be coming to school that day. She thanked me for letting her know and passed it on to the Kindergarten teacher.

After a long unnerving morning, our lunch hour finally arrived. I dressed as quickly as possible and headed home for lunch. Upon arriving home I immediately asked how my sister was doing. Mom replied that she was in bed resting because she fell on the sidewalk on the way to school. That was when I laid the news on her that she was hit by a car.

That's when all heck broke loose. A whole new educational moment began to unfold. This young first grader learned that he should have come home with his sister immediately. Also, it would have been all right to talk with the stranger that drove the car and gotten his license plate number.

My mother had me stay home the rest of that afternoon. A policeman was summoned and unfortunately was not able to glean enough information to help. Needless to say, lectures abounded over this incident. Bottom line was that my sister was not seriously injured in spite of having a bruised hip for awhile. The school year continued with no further negative events.

Like most schools today, our school had it's fair share of fund raisers. One such exploit that occurred in the Spring of 1948 was the sale of vegetable seed packets for five cents each. Mom had given me a dime and allowed me to purchase two packets of seeds. The choice was all mine so I opted for carrots and peas.

Dad always tilled a small area in the back yard for some tomato plants. Once the weather was favorable enough for planting Dad put my seeds in the ground along the edge of the garden. Each morning as I headed for school I would check for plants. Eventually, I saw the round peas coming up out of the ground so I would push them back down. A couple of days later, the same thing again. One evening at the supper table Dad mentioned he noticed that the plants were popping out and then disappeared. We all had a good laugh when I revealed that I had thought they were falling out and needed to be replanted. Later that growing season we all had some fresh peas early on and plenty of carrots later in Fall.

Another such event we were introduced to in our young first-grade years was Fire Prevention Week. Early in the week we were instructed to remove all our books and belongings from our desk storage compartments and throw out any excess loose paper. We were taught what combustibles were and took home information for our parents.

During the week we experienced a fire drill and learned how to safely evacuate the school building. Our teacher was very pleased with our mastery of fire safety.

One major event was yet to occur unannounced - a visit to each room by an unsavory character named Fiery Felix (a high school student dressed in costume). Rumors abounded that Fiery Felix would light desks on fire if he found scrap paper sticking out of the storage compartments.

In the middle of class one morning the moment we all dreaded had arrived. There was a soft tapping on the classroom door. Our teacher opened it and in walked Fiery Felix, a tall red cat with whiskers and a tail. He held a bundle of foot-long matches in one hand and his tail in the other. He prowled around the room and looked down all the aisles. As he slowly headed back toward the door we all yelled in unison: "Get out of here Fiery Felix, this is a clean room." He made a snarly cat sound and left for the next room. We had succeeded in avoiding the wrath of Fiery Felix.

Summer was gaining on us rapidly. The school year was again coming to an end. While my sister was preparing for her Kindergarten graduation exercise, I was busy taking my very first final exams. My sister finished Kindergarten and would now be entering a full day of classes in the fall season. I passed First Grade and would be traveling upstairs for my Second Grade classes next school semester. Again, we all said goodbye for the summer.

SUMMER OF '48

Summer always seemed to start out with nice sunny weather and this summer was no exception. I had a metal wagon that I received as a birthday gift that year and my sister had a new tricycle. The sidewalks became our roadways. Even though we were confined to Steuben Street only, the sidewalks had enough dips and bumps to keep the excitement high.

Without any of today's inventions we still managed to create our own wholesome fun. Something exciting was always on the horizon.

Empty beer and soda bottle hunts were always near the top of the list of things to do. One bottle was all we ever needed to find. A quick trip to the corner store at Steuben and Kirkpatrick Streets would net a quick two cent refund. This would be enough to purchase two Bazooka bubble gums, a two- pack of Mary Jane candy, or a pair of miniature wax bottles each containing a sweet, colored syrup.

Rain or shine, each day was an adventure. On rainy days Mom would bring out old Montgomery Ward catalogs and scissors. My sister and I would sit for hours cutting things out of the catalog to glue on sheets of paper and create stories. After awhile we would resort to what we called: "Making spices." We would take newspapers and cut them into thin strips about a half inch wide. We would then cut these strips into small squares and keep them in an old cigar box. Mom thought it was cute until she found remnants scattered around the house.

Mom and Dad always liked fishing together. One Saturday afternoon they loaded us into the '36 Chevy and drove to one of their favorite fishing spots along the river near Euclid, New York. They taught us the basics of fishing that day. I don't think my sister cared for it that much, but I did.

While we were fishing that day someone accidentally hit and injured a beagle dog that belonged to a man in a nearby house. The dog was limping and barking as it circled around my sister and me. Mom and Dad told us to sit very still and wait. Eventually, the dog ran off into a wooded area. Soon after that we packed up and went home.

Two sights and sounds that were ever present daily were those of the huckster and scissors grinder. Hucksters would drive medium size trucks loaded with arrays of fruits and vegetables down the various streets. A couple of men would walk behind the truck hollering out the various items available. A spring scale hung dangling from a metal bar that spanned the wooden side racks. When housewives would approach, the truck would stop long enough for the huckster to transact the sale and then move on.

The scissors grinder was generally an older man. He would walk down the sidewalks ringing a large handheld bell to alert housewives that he was available to sharpen their knives and scissors. He carried a stone grinding wheel attached to a heavy metal frame on his back using shoulder straps. When someone came out with implements that needed sharpening, he would lower his grinder to the sidewalk, pump a pedal with his foot to spin the stone, and grind away while we got to see the sparks fly. When finished, he would collect his coin for the work, heft the grinding wheel onto his back, and continue ringing his bell as he strolled away looking for his next customer.

Since swimming at local pools was disallowed because of the polio scare, we had other ways to cool off on hot summer days. My sister and I each had a large metal washtub. We would bring these outside, set them on a level spot near the back door, and fill them with water from the garden hose. After donning our swimsuits, we would splash around for hours. Playing with our squirt guns always added and additional element of excitement.

Once in a while we would all drive to a beach called Boysen's Bay located on Oneida Lake to swim. Mom and Dad liked this beach because it was small and not very crowded. The ride there took us over South Bay Road and through a very dingy area known as the Cicero Swamp. The swamp encompassed a large volume of land and was densely populated with large trees. It looked like the perfect setting for a swamp monster movie. My sister and I would make each other offers of large sums of money to walk through this area and exit on the other side, wherever that might be. Neither one of us ever agreed to accept the challenge for any amount of money.

There was a short period of time when Mom had to enter the hospital for abdominal surgery. My sister and I were to stay with Mom and Dad's friends named Eva and Ray for approximately one week.

Eva and Ray lived on the opposite side of Syracuse, somewhat distant from the Steuben Street area. They had two older daughters and an infant son. The two older daughters would take turns playing with my sister and me. They would take us to a school playground near their home where we could slide and swing. They were very nice children.

Eva was a very caring type person and always treated us nicely. Ray was a hard working man with gentle qualities. Being as young as my sister and I were, we did not fully understand why Mom was in the hospital.

During our first evening at the supper table Ray announced to us that Mom had her surgery and was doing very well. He also told us that he and Dad had each donated a unit of blood to the Red Cross Organization that very day and it would be swapped for two units of blood for our mother. Not fully understanding what was happening, I later realized that the sacrifice Ray made for Mom's well being was exemplary.

Behind Eva and Ray's home was a small wooded area at the edge of a sizable field. A few of the neighborhood children had made a teepee-shaped fort out of a blanket and some wooden tree branches. They would use this fort for shade while reading comic books. Not too far away from the fort was a junk pile that contained items discarded from various homes in the neighborhood.

The day had finally arrived when Dad would be picking my sister and me up to go back home. We both felt that Eva and Ray had been so good to us that we wanted to do something for them in appreciation for their kindness. As we sat on their back porch trying to come up with a good idea, we noticed that the porch floor was faded and quite worn down. Then, like a flash of light, my sister and I both agreed on the perfect parting gift.

Moments later, we were at the junk heap picking out a half-full can of used paint along with a couple of brushes. The paint was a creamy-yellow color and we felt that would be perfect for the job.

We quickly returned to the back porch, opened the paint can, and started painting the floor from the farthest corner toward the steps. We had only a few boards left to finish when the paint can was empty. We both got up to return the brushes and can back to the junk pile.

As fate would have it, there stood Dad at the bottom of the steps wanting to know what the heck we thought we were doing. The moment became quite embarrassing. Dad immediately marched us into the house and made us explain to Eva and Ray what we had done. Thinking the worst was about to happen, Ray looked down at us and advised us not to worry about it.

Even though we were verbally pounded back home, I always felt that Ray really did appreciate our gesture of gratitude. Anyway, I hope so.

Throughout the summer months posters would appear on telephone poles announcing festivals and carnivals. Although these were fun filled events their main purpose was to make money. It was a rare occasion when we would attend such events.

One summer day the Assumption Church parish was holding their annual festival on their school yard property directly behind the church. Mom and Dad decided to take us there for a little while. We walked down Steuben Street to the corner and then down Pond Street a couple of blocks to the school. As we entered the courtyard Mom told us we could take one chance on a game. She picked the fish pond booth because we were guaranteed a prize. We paid our nickel and each of us received some sort of trinket. It was a small event so it was not long before we trudged back up the hill and went home.

At another time we piled into the car with our parents and Dad drove to Liverpool. When we arrived the sight was almost too good to be true. This was the first time I ever saw a full-blown carnival. Liverpool had a large triangular-shaped park in the middle of the village and it was filled with lights, rides, and booths of all sorts. Dad parked and we crossed the street entering this fabulous wonderland.

Our very first ride was on the carousel. My sister and I rode side-by- side on horses that moved up-and-down as the carousel rotated. We were fascinated. Following the carousel, we had rides in small cars that also chased each other in a circle.

After seeing everything there, our day finally ended with a box of popcorn and an abundance of memories to take back home.

AUTOMOBILES

⁓

During the late 1940's very few families residing on Steuben Street had automobiles. Since most of the Steuben Street homes were constructed around the year 1900, many were without driveways nor room to add one.

My father owned a 1936 two-door Chevrolet that was a flat dark blue color. Since horse-drawn wagons were still around in the 1940's, flat paint on automobiles minimized reflections that could possible spook a horse and cause an accident.

Although automobiles provided convenient transport they required considerable time-consuming upkeep compared to the vehicles of today.

The biggest inconvenience was a flat tire. Tires back then all had inner tubes inside. The inner tubes were donut-shaped rubber bladders that held the air inside each tire. They were prone to developing leaks quite often. Along with the usual nail-in-the-street, small pebbles inside the tire would wear a hole in the tube. In addition, the tubes would tend to shift causing a pinch in the rubber also resulting in an air leak.

Automobile trunks were much larger in the older cars. Being that flat tires were somewhat chronic, Dad always carried three spare tires in the trunk along with a round cylindrical container of tube patches and rubber cement.

Quite often Dad would check all the spare tires to make sure they were inflated. He and I would spend a Saturday morning every couple of months fixing the flat ones. This was not a simple operation. The tire was laid flat on the ground. We would stand on the tire and use the heels of our shoes to release the tire from the metal rim all the way around. A special flat bar called a tire iron was then used to carefully pry one side of the tire from behind the rim to the outside. Then, the tube was extracted from within.

Once removed from the tire, air was hand pumped (no small compressors back then) into the tube to locate the leak. Sometimes the leak was so small that a washtub of water had to be used to find it. Once located, the leaky area was washed, dried, roughed-up with a special scratching tool (usually built into the cover of the repair kit), brushed with rubber cement, and covered with a patch. The patch was pressed in place until the cement had set.

To complete the job, the tube was partially inflated just enough to get it around the metal rim, back into the time, and positioned for the air valve to properly locate. The flat tire iron was then used to draw the inside rim of the tire back over the metal rim. Once this was completed the tire was inflated fully using a hand pump only. It was then set aside for a day or so for verification that it no longer leaked.

Yes, the inevitable did happen. Once in awhile a repaired tire would still leak. Again, the whole process needed to be repeated. Back then the tire quality exhibited today was only a fantasy.

We did not use our car everyday. If within walking distance, we walked. Many days Dad walked to work because the car did not start or he was waiting for the weekend or a nice day to replace a defective part. Lucky for us Dad was mechanically inclined. He was good at finding replacement parts at the junk yard or using his tool and die making skills to fabricate a part.

Automobiles of that vintage could be hard-starting. The six-volt batteries were difficult to keep charged and often resulted in cars not starting. Our car had a hand crank that slid into an opening in the front grille. I remember Dad used it quite often to start the engine when the battery was low. During the winter months he would hand-crank the engine a few times to free it up before using the electric starter. Many winter mornings I headed out the back door for school only to find the hand crank inserted and Dad's foot tracks headed out the driveway as he did not get the car started and walked to work instead.

The summertime presented a slightly different situation known as overheating. Dad always carried two one-gallon glass jugs of water in the trunk during the summer months. Plastic jugs did not exist at that time. Automobile engines would overheat easily during summer. My father would always remove the thermostat so the cooling system would not boil over. The water he carried was added at regular intervals to replace water that had boiled away. Permanent antifreeze fluid was just coming out into the market but was very expensive. Water seemed to serve the purpose quite well. Alcohol blended with the water was used as an antifreeze during wintertime.

Winter driving was always a challenge. The north side area around Steuben Street contains a fair share of hills. The streets were narrow. Even though snow plow drivers did their best, a lot of slush was always present. On many days chains around both rear tires were necessary in order to navigate the streets. It was not uncommon to hear the rhythmic clanking of tire chains on both cars and trucks during the snowiest weeks of the season.

One sunny afternoon Dad took us for a ride while he ran some errands. Near the end of the trip he drove down Wolf Street, rounded the corner onto Spring Street, and parked the car along the curb. Dad told us to stay in the back seat and not to touch anything. He then left the car and went directly into the corner store to pick up a small item.

My sister and I decided this would be a good opportunity to see what driving was all about. Within seconds we were over the seat backs and into the front seat. I positioned myself behind the steering wheel while she sat in the right front seat. I moved the steering wheel from left to right pretending we were driving. This particular section of Spring Street had a slight downward slope that was aimed a the old ballpark a block away.

Moments after commenting to my sister that I wondered how Dad made this go, she jiggled the gearshift lever that sat centered between the driver and passenger seats. While commenting on how she saw Dad move it, with one quick jerk it was dislodged to a neutral position. To our amazement the car started to slowly roll down the street. Lucky for us a young man in a NAVY uniform came running across the street and stopped the car from moving any further. Within seconds Dad returned to find the NAVY man intently holding the door post on the driver's side. Dad thanked him profusely, got in the car, ordered us back onto the rear seat, and proceeded back home.

Dad figured we learned our lesson. On the other hand Mom thought that was not enough as she yelled and opened up what is affectionately known as a can of butt whopping.

SECOND GRADE

～

Summer was so much fun that the start of school again in the Fall of 1948 seemed like an invasion. Even so, it was exciting to be heading back in the classroom.

One of our back-to-school rituals included a trip to the shoe store. We always looked forward to a new pair of shoes for the upcoming school year. Our old pair then became our play shoes and replaced the worn pair that we doctored form the previous year. As always, the trip to the shoe store was to be taken seriously. Utility was first and foremost. What appealed to the eye was more than likely rejected as low quality.

The highlight of the trip was using the X-ray machine and observing our foot bones as the salesman and our parents would check for proper fit. We would step up on a small platform at the base of the X-ray machine, slide our feet forward into a narrow opening, and peer into one of three visors located on the top. The other two visors were for a parent and the salesman. Once in position, the salesman would push a button to activate the machine. A soft green glow would manifest itself in the machine and the skeleton of our feet would appear for a few seconds. Once home we had the privilege of wearing our new shoes around the house for a few hours to break them in before school started.

I was starting Second Grade and my sister was entering First Grade.

Mom must have been elated that we were both now in all day sessions. She would still need to endure our lunch hour at home each day though.

The classroom was located on the second floor above the Kindergarten and First Grade rooms. I entered the school via the same door and immediately climbed a long staircase. Feeling like older pupils now, my classmates and I were quickly alerted to the fact that we all needed to act that way and set a good example for the younger students. Of course, the wise thing to do was taking that advice seriously.

Our Second Grade teacher was named Sister Augustine. We all quickly realized that this year would be filled with academic challenges of all sorts. Spelling words were longer and harder to spell. Arithmetic involved addition of three and four place numbers as well as subtraction. English led us to a basic understanding of sentence structure as well as developing sentences that included use of the new words we learned during Spelling class. I was sent home many times with words that I needed to look up the meanings of in a book called a dictionary.

As members of the Catholic Church, the Second Grade class prepared for making our First Holy Communion in May of 1949.

Religion classes were included in our studies at St. John the Baptist Academy. The Catholic Church believed children seven years of age were considered to have reached the age of reason. This signifies that a child of seven is mature enough to differentiate between good and evil and therefor may be eligible to receive additional Sacraments in the Church.

Attendance at Mass every Sunday morning was required in order to assure Christianity would prevail throughout each week in our lives. Once old enough to understand the Sacraments of Penance and Holy Communion, Church members seek the privilege of receive these Sacraments on a regular basis.

We studied hard and looked forward to our seasonal holidays like Columbus Day, Armistice Day, Thanksgiving, and Christmas. Before long we were into the beginning of the year 1949. As Spring arrived we were well into preparation for receiving our First Holy Communion. Boys needed to purchase white suits, neckties, and shoes for the occasion. Girls were fitted for white formal dresses and veils.

Easter arrived on April seventeenth that year. We celebrated with Mass that Sunday morning before returning home to our Easter baskets and a big chocolate bunny. Mom always prepared a baked ham for dinner while she listened to the Polish Polka Hour on the radio.

Another week of school had passed. The following weekend had barely started when Mom received a phone call. We all piled into the car and headed to the Galeville store. Mom was in tears.

Arriving at the store, Dad parked behind it near the rear entrance. A local physician named Dr. Bryant had arrived minutes earlier. My grandma Bugnacki had had a stroke while working in the store that morning and was lying on the floor. My sister and I sat in the car for a long while. At one point I saw my Mom, Dad, Dr. Bryant, and an uncle carrying Grandma from the store and up the rear staircase to her bed. After awhile, Dad took us kids home and Mom stayed for awhile longer.

Grandma Bugnacki passed away that Sunday morning exactly one week after Easter. The kind lady with the beautiful smile had departed this life forever.

Second Grade was difficult to finish. I was only a couple of weeks away from making my First Communion and my Grandma would not be here to see it. Mom assured me that I would see her again someday.

May eventually arrived and my Second Grade classmates and I made our First Communion. We celebrated at home with a cake Mom had baked specifically for the occasion.

Mid-June of 1949 arrived and my class was taking written tests that, once graded, would solidify our promotion into Third Grade that upcoming Fall. Once our morning exam was completed, we had an extended lunch break before returning for another exam in the afternoon.

One particular day we arrived home midday and Mom met us on the front porch. She had us com in the sitting room door instead of the usual back door entry. She informed us that her and Dad had a big surprise for us.

She took us to the back door and opened it. There in the yard sat a wooden fishing boat on a small metal trailer. The boat had four seats, one for each of us. It's bottom was painted green and the sides were white. This was only part of the marvel. They had also purchased a small piece of land on Oneida Lake where the boat could be kept during the summer months. But, there would be no fishing trips until exams were over and passing grades were received.

It appeared that a wing-ding of a summer was on the horizon. The excitement was close to overwhelming.

SUMMER OF '49

Summer was evolving into a season for deep breaths and sighs of relief. School was starting to become more work than fun. This two and one- half month respite seemed to grow shorter and shorter with age. However, the precious months were here again for our enjoyment.

This particular summer started out with new exploration around the Steuben Street area. I had received a new scooter for my birthday that April and was now given permission to circle the block. My favorite route took me down the sidewalks of Steuben, around the corner onto the downward slope of Kirkpatrick Street, a scary speed reduction to make the turn onto Alvord Street, a straight run down Alvord to Pond St., then an uphill climb on Pond back to Steuben Street. After a short rest on our front steps I was off again on a similar run in the opposite direction.

I always felt that my sister and I were quite well behaved. We were mostly polite and obedient. However, on occasion we did manage to get into mischief. When that happened, Mom would step in and determine a punishment suitable for the type of infraction committed.

One of her favorite enforcement's was placing a chair in an area we referred to as the kitchen corner. Upon being instructed to sit there, we were given a time duration appropriate to the offense we were to be punished for committing. And so, the long confinement would commence.

After awhile I discovered a way to circumvent some of the punishment time. During a moment of brilliance I decided that a bathroom break would be just the ticket to freedom. When the right moment arrived, I did announce that I desperately needed a bathroom break. Mom happily consented and off the chair I would fly to my moments of freedom. If swift enough, I could manage to snatch a comic book along the way.

Feeling like a winner, I would enter the bathroom with the zeal of a winner momentarily. Mom would belch out one last instruction to leave the bathroom door ajar slightly so she could hear that I really needed to go.

Now, it began to look like this was turning into a real sticky situation that would require some fast thinking. While glancing quickly at the sink, the idea struck like lightning. The only solution was to run the faucet ever so slow and capture a quantity of water in cupped hands. This water was then dribbled over the toilet bowl in a slow fashion to simulate a natural sounding event.

It turned out that this procedure did the trick. Although never seeming to be suspicious, Mom would always make sure I returned back the the chair.

Eventually, sitting in the corner became a thing of the past and was replaced by other restrictions instead. I never realized until later in life that Mom fell for this trick so deeply.

Mom would take great pride in passing her chair-sitting discipline theory on to her sisters. She would always add the importance of leaving the bathroom door ajar and listen if a bathroom break was necessary.

This was one carefully guarded secret that was never revealed in the Steuben Street bungalow. Unbeknown to us children, Mom and Dad purchased a small lot on the west end of Oneida lake where they planned on keeping our new boat for the summer. The lot was located in the southwest corner of a small cove that sat along the north side of Milton Point on Oneida Lake. Access to the lot was from a small dirt road called John Street. As best I recall, the lot was very narrow and the shore was somewhat rocky. The water was very shallow near the shoreline but ramped off to several feet deep a little way out.

Once the boat was on the water it stayed there the whole summer season. Dad drove a large pipe in the ground about thirty feet out from the shore. The boat was moored to this pipe with a short rope from it's bow. The back end of the boat was tied to a tree on the shore. This allowed the boat to float freely during weather changes and while we were away at home.

One of Dad's favorite fishing spots was in an area named Big Bay. It was directly north of our cove. Initially, we did not have a motor on the boat. We would row the boat out to a fishing area. On calm days I would get to row for awhile. I really enjoyed that.

After awhile Dad purchased a small outboard motor. This motor was silver colored and was not the easiest to get running. Starting the motor involved using a short rope that wrapped around the flywheel atop the motor and pulled briskly. Many times it took several rewraps and pulls to finally effect a start.

Although the boat had four seats, my sister and I would always ride side-by-side in the front seat. On calm days we could look directly ahead of the boat and down into the clear water. Many times we watched large snapping turtles scramble for the depths as the boat would approach them.

The fish we caught were mostly perch and sunfish. Occasionally, Mom or Dad would catch a nice small mouth or largemouth bass. We would fish the lily pad area near the western shoreline of Big Bay on many occasions. The bobbers we used in these shallow areas were corks that Dad had saved from vinegar jugs. He wold drill a hole directly down the center of the cork, make a slit down the side with a small saw, and carve a wood peg from a tree branch to fit the long center hole. The cork would then be slid over the fish line and adjusted to the proper position for the water depth in the area. Once positioned the line was wrapped through the slit in the cork and held in position with friction by inserting the peg into the top of the hole.

From this time on, fishing became a big part of our childhood. I had learned how to properly clean the fish we caught. Oneida Lake fish became a major staple in our household. Eventually, Mom purchased a deep fryer specifically for cooking the fish.

At some point I had received a pair of hip boots. This meant that I could walk out into the water far enough to reach the boat and bail the water out after a rainfall. I would also walk out from the shore and try my luck at fishing in the cove.

Learning to fish was one thing. Learning to cast a line to a specific spot on the water turned out to be much more demanding. Many summer hours were spent in the backyard on Steuben Street learning how to cast. My father would leave me a couple of used inner tubes from his old tires. I would pump them up with a hand pump and position them in various spots throughout the back yard. After attaching a lead sinker to my line, I would practice aiming at the inner tubes when casting my line. It took awhile to hit the targets almost every time but eventually I developed the skill.

Many of our previous summer activities took second place to having a boat and going fishing. At some point that year the old 1936 Chevy needed to be replaced. It had become quite rusty and a little unreliable.

We were excited the day we drove over to pick up our next car. It was a black four-door sedan. Even though it looked much newer inside and out it was another 1936 Chevy. Dad bought it from the Thompson boat dealer where he had purchased the boat. The car even had a large oval Thompson decal on the outside of both front doors. Compared to the old car, this one rode like brand new.

The old car went up on blocks in the Steuben Street backyard for awhile as Dad found it to be a smorgasbord or spare parts that could be used if needed. Eventually, Dad gave it to someone who showed up with a set of tires and towed it away. Although Dad was getting rid of junk, another gentleman had found his treasure.

Steuben Street residents seemed to have a lot of pride in keeping the neighborhood clean and tidy. However, even the best efforts could not seem to control the stray cat population. Dad was always complaining about the smell around the cellar windows because male cats always seemed to spray in those areas. Another problem was finding litters of kittens living under the front porch. At the proper time they needed to be rounded up and taken to the SPCA animal shelter to be put up for adoption. Dad was never in a good disposition when these events would occur under our porch.

My sister and I were instructed not to play with stray cats. Most of the time we complied with this unwritten household law. On one occasion, my sister and I were playing a couple of houses away from ours when a medium-size stray kitten showed up on the scene. Knowing the stray cat rule, my sister decided to play with the cat anyway. After about fifteen minutes of fun, she decided to tie a balloon and string to the cat's tail. Soon afterward the cat ran across the street and began roaming the neighborhood, balloon and all.

We were soon called in to wash for supper. Sitting down to eat always seemed to be the most appropriate time to tattle. I could not resist spilling the beans about the cat with the balloon attached.

Mom and Dad were quick to blame us both, one for doing it and the other for watching and not stopping it. When supper was over, Dad immediately took to the street to locate the cat. After about twenty minutes Dad returned with the cat, took out his small pocket knife, cut the string from the tail, and freed the cat.

Dad was furious when he came back into the house and we ended up in bed early that evening.

From time to time I still have visions of that day watching Dad walking down the sidewalk of Steuben Street with a cat tucked under his arm and a balloon floating around on a short string. I can't help but chuckle.

By the end of summer I was beginning to grasp what owning a boat was all about and that was one thing, work. If there was significant rain during the week, the boat would need bailing out since it had no cover on it. My job was to put on the hip boots, wade out to the boat with tin cans and a sponge, and bail the water until the inside was dry again.

For us, summer ended when school was starting. This meant that the boat had to be trailered and towed back home for the winter. Once home, it was turned over and lifted onto saw horses where it would rest until the springtime scraping and painting would commence.

School would be starting again soon and fishing would become a thing-of-the-past until the next summer season arrived. One of the most memorable events of this summer for me was Binky.

The author and his sister Elaine anchored at the cove near Milton point in 1949

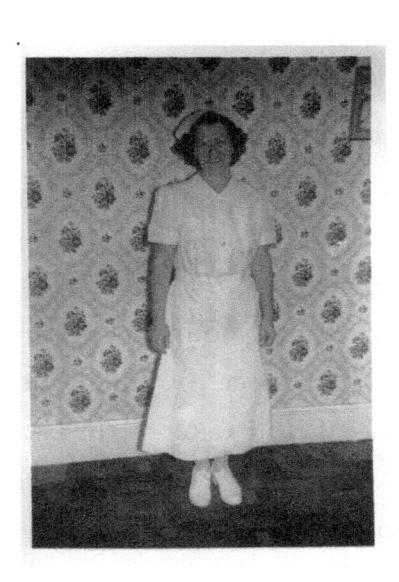

The author's mother Helen in the Steuben Street sitting room in 1949.

BINKY

It was a bright sunny day as our boat maneuvered in an eastward direction from the small bay near Milton Point where it was moored. The seven and one-half horsepower outboard roared to life at Dad's third pull of the starter rope. I quickly put the oars into their proper place, climbed past my mother, and took my position in the front seat alongside my sister.

Once seated, I gave my Dad a glance that he quickly interpreted. The throttle on the motor was gradually opened until full power was realized. The front of the boat rose slightly as the ten mile-per-hour speed was attained.

At this very early morning hour the surface of Oneida Lake was smooth as satin. Looking over the small deck we could see into the depths of the crystal clear water as the boat gracefully rounded the point and headed westward on into Big Bay. The assortment of weeds passing under the boat gave me the sensation of flying over tree tops. Several hundred feet in the distance bobbed the inky black noses of snapping turtles lazily digesting their breakfasts.

My sister and I would point in excitement if it appeared we may be on a collision course with one of these magnificent creatures. Somehow, Dad knew just where to navigate and always managed it perfectly, affording the opportunity of observing these reptiles at a close distance. In every instance these "snappers" demonstrated their strength and agility by using their powerful web-fingered claws to dive deep and quickly disappear from sight.

As we approached the innermost shore of the bay, Dad gradually closed the throttle of the motor until it coughed to a stop. Very quietly he would use the oars to approach the vicinity of the lily pads. Each of us would then bait our hooks, adjust our cork bobbers, and cast our lines toward the lily pads. Dad never spoke much while fishing but the look on his face was one of anticipation of perhaps catching a large fish, possibly a nice bass. That is, before my sister and I would become bored and get so unruly that our antics would result in excessive noise and scare all the fish away.

Well, this particular day fishing was not very good. We were catching very small sunfish and perch only. Needless to say, my sister and I were becoming restless earlier than usual. Suddenly, Dad asked for the landing net. It seemed a bit strange since he had already set his fishing pole down in the boat. I handed him the net and watched as he scooped it into the water. You can only imagine our surprise when he lifted the net from the water and swung it back into the boat. It contained a small colorful turtle no bigger around than a silver dollar.

We all took turns holding the turtle while taking great care to avoid any injury to it. It's head, legs, and tail remained retracted tightly against it's shell while making the rounds among us several times. After a short while we placed the turtle into a small, clean tin can containing a small amount of water. Only once did the turtle extend it's head momentarily for a quick peek at us.

That day became a special day because we actually headed home with the turtle as our new adopted pet. There was one major stipulation, it was ours for the summer only. When Fall arrived the turtle was to be returned to it's natural habitat in time to dig in and hibernate for the winter months.

Yep! We both agreed to that thinking that things could change and everyone would forget about the stipulation.

I don't think our eyes left the contents of that tin can all the rest of that day. Each time we would observe the head extend slightly we would pick the turtle up and hold it in hopes that it would want to play with us. That did not seem to work very well. The turtle was just too scared or smart, I was not sure which of the two, probably a little of both. No name we came up with sounded suitable until my sister suggested the name Binky. That was it. The turtle's name was now officially Binky.

When we arrived back home that day, Dad suggested we take a cardboard box and line it with newspaper for Binky to live in. Once that was done Dad provided us with a large metal ice cube tray to fill with water for Binky's very own pond. We were then sent scurrying outside to locate some small stones. The small stones were then arranged around both the inside and outside of the ice cube tray so Binky could easily enter and leave the water.

I had not realized it at the time, but Dad sure seemed to know a whole lot about turtles.

Once Binky's home was prepared we placed him in it. Per Mom's instruction the box was to be kept in the back room and out of the way of normal daily activity. After a short while, Binky began to relax and move about. Binky seemed to adapt well to his new home. He was in and out of his pond quite regularly and always appeared to enjoy resting on one flat stone in particular. Dad showed us how to turn up small rocks around the garden perimeter and locate small earthworms that Binky enjoyed for meals. Further into the summer months we found that worms were becoming scarce. Dad brought the wrath of Mom to life by suggesting we catch houseflies for Binky to eat.

When it came to Binky we must have been doing everything perfect. Binky thrived very well under our care. Once over his shyness he would showoff his strength by climbing on our hands and arms. Although very tiny, his claws could be felt through our clothing.

As summer days slid into late August we reached a time when finding food for Binky became a time consuming challenge. In the mid of our frustration, it was Dad to the rescue again. He demonstrated how Binky would tear into a sliver of raw hamburger. I remember how hard he laughed when I mentioned how nice it would have been to know that much sooner.

In no time at all my sister and I were back in school again. How exciting it was to tell our friends about Binky. A special few even got to meet Binky.

Then, before we realized it, October was here. I'll never forget that feeling I had that Columbus Day morning when Dad announced that it was time for Binky to return to the lake. I had totally forgotten that long ago agreement we made the day we adopted Binky.

The trip to our lot on the lake seemed like the fastest ever. My sister and I walked to the shore and said out goodbye to Binky. We took turns holding him one last time. I lowered my hand down just under the surface of the water. Binky walked off my open palm and began to swim away from the shore with his head held high. I felt sad watching him leave. Binky was about fifteen feet from shore when he stopped, turned around, and looked back as if to say his goodbye. In an instant he was paddling again out toward deeper water. Another five minutes or so he was out of sight.

As the long winter months were passing I remember asking Dad what he thought Binky was doing. He would assure me that Binky was burrowed underground in the lake hibernating until Spring with the rest of the turtles.

It was around midwinter of that year when I came to realize that I would never see Binky again. As a young lad I hoped we had done the right thing. Binky always seemed so happy with us. I guess that was the first time I actually realized that you have something or someone only for awhile, then they go on to fulfill the existence that they were created for.

Even today when I see turtles at a pet store or the zoo, I always wonder what became of Binky and how he felt about his summer with people so long ago.

Who knows, maybe Binky tells his story too.

THIRD GRADE

Third Grade started out much like previous years had begun. For some reason things did not quite harmonize with me quite the same this school season.

My teacher's name was Sister Irmena. Right from the start she had some oddities about her that seemed to ruffle me. Maybe it was me. Maybe it was her. But, it seemed like we just started off on the wrong foot and stayed that way for most of the year.

My sister was now in Second Grade and the classroom was directly across the hall from mine. Sister Irmena quickly developed a propensity for sending home notes about me with my sister. This caused a lot of tension at home for me.

Apparently my dress code was an issue. We were to start wearing long-sleeve dress shirts. Mom bought long-sleeve shirts for me but they were polo shirts and not dress shirts. I was criticized on a daily basis for not wearing proper shirts. A note would go home and the message I was to deliver back to school was nothing a young child could repeat in public, much less in a Catholic school.

We were not a rich family by any means. Dad worked very hard for what he was paid each week. Mom was taking first-aid classes at the Red Cross office down on Genesee Street so she could work part time as a nurses aide. We did have a small fishing boat but that was to keep us supplied with fresh fish during the summer season.

For me the messages were somewhat scrambled. Fighting in school was prohibited. Unfortunately, there were bullies. It upset me to have to deal with some of them. They were sneaky and generally did not get caught. If the teacher did not see an incident, they were prone to disregard it and dub the offended party a tattletale which was also frowned upon. The advice from home was to make a fist and smash the instigator in the nose. You can image just what that would lead to.

So, for me this was truly starting out to be a year of turmoil. On the brighter side, we began to learn cursive writing. We had a small orange book called a Palmer Method book that we used to develop our alphabet and help us work toward good penmanship.

Along with cursive writing came the ink pen. Each desk had a two-inch diameter hole located at the upper right-hand corner of our desks. We had received small glass bottles of ink that sat in these holes. The ink bottles had a cork stopper in the top that had to be removed ever so carefully when used. When properly placed in the desk these bottles of ink became known as ink wells.

Initially, we would practice our cursive writing with a lead pencil and then with a pen that had to be dipped into the ink. Extreme care was demanded when ink was being used. We were especially vulnerable if a girl with long hair sat directly in front of us. Thank goodness I never had to deal with that situation.

At some point during that year we began changing over to using fountain pens. Fountain pens were designed to hold a small quantity of ink that allowed the pen to write for an extended period without needing to be dipped in an ink well. The ink was stored in a long thin rubber bladder inside the pen. A small lever on the side of the pen for filling it could be pulled up and released to draw ink into the storage bladder. A metal bullet-shaped cover went over the end to protect the pen tip itself. This metal cover had a clip on the side so the pen could be carried in a shirt pocket.

By now the danger should start becoming obvious. If the pen is filled with ink and the filler lever on the side is accidentally pulled, the ink will empty immediately. Unfortunately, we had one class bully that specialized in grabbing pens form pockets and draining the ink into the pen cover ruining shirts and anything else that got dripped on. This was never dealt with appropriately and my advise from home was of course: "Punch him in the nose every time he does it."

Not too far into the school year my mother had to break down and conform to the school dress code for boys. I finally had dress shirts and pants to wear. Thinking of my growth spurts, Mom bought dress shirts with sleeves longer than normal so they would fit me the following year. As a result I had to wear arm bands above my elbows to hold the sleeves up far enough to prevent soiling. Needless to say, I was the only boy in class that looked like a western movie bartender. Again, I received my share of teasing bordering on ridicule.

It seemed that I was always in some sort of conflict with my teacher that year. Over time I mentioned these concerns to my mother, her response was: "You better study hard so you pass or you will have that same teacher for another year if you don't."

It was becoming quite apparent that changes happen continuously throughout life and it seemed like this was a banner year in the making. Our bungalow on Steuben Street became my haven and I loved every minute of living there.

Dad had worked at a company named Cine-Simplex all during the war years. After some consolidations, Cine-Simplex made the decision to shut down their operation in Syracuse and move it to another facility out of this state. Since we were in no position to uproot and move to another location, Dad was laid off from his job.

I remember on his last day of work at Cine-Simplex he arrived home with his tool boxes. He carried them in one-by-one and lined them up against the wall in the back room. I felt sad for him. He was a quiet man. He never showed it but I knew he must have felt something inside.

After interviews at a few prospective companies, Dad was offered a job in the tool room as a tool and die maker at the Easy Washing Machine Company on Spencer Street here in Syracuse. He loaded his tools into the '36 Chevy and headed back to work on the evening shift.

Around that same time, Mom had finished her first-aid courses and started a part-time job as a nurse's aide at Saint Joseph's

Hospital located on Prospect Ave. here in Syracuse. She alternated working evenings and days. Many Saturday evenings we had to stay awake until eleven o'clock and ride up there with Dad to pick her up after work.

When Mom was later assigned to work days, she was offered the opportunity to take the state licensing exam to qualify as a Practical Nurse. She passed with flying colors. On December 8, 1949 she received her certificate as a Licensed Practical Nurse in the State of New York.

The furniture in our Steuben Street parlor was quickly rearranged to provide wall space so Dad could photograph her in her nurses uniform holding her license. We were all proud of the little girl from Galeville that only got to Sixth Grade in school and was now a Licensed Practical Nurse.

Back in school we were preparing for the Christmas Season. Each year we would erect a Christmas Tree in the classroom. Generally, one of the students would donate a tree and we would all bring in some sort of ornament to place on it.

Like everything else that year, the tree decorations had to be different. Our teacher decided that there would be no ornaments on the tree. Only silver foil icicles were to adorn the branches. To me, this was weird. Our classroom tree did not display the color and warmth I had fondly associated with the secular side of the Christmas season. As a matter of fact, the tree looked like a silver colored teepee.

Although the holiday season passed in uneventful fashion, needless to say my sister and I approached Spring with a good case of the Chicken Pox. I never itched so much in my life as I did that particular week. Only a short while later we polished off our childhood disease list by contacting both the measles and mumps. I was beginning to think there really was such a thing as a Third Grade Curse.

Many families come into contact with neighborhood acquaintances that become great friends forever. One such family that I was privileged to know was the Reimold family.

My father grew up around the corner from Steuben street and attended school with a friend named Carl Reimold who lived a few houses away. Carl grew up and married a very nice lady named Gertrude. They had two lovely daughters, Carol and Lynda. Carol was about my age and Lynda a few years younger.

One day my sister and I spent the afternoon at their house on Hood Avenue. It was during the winter months and we had been making snow figures in the back yard. Another young boy in the neighborhood stopped by and we started a game of Hide-and-Seek.

The Reimold's had a detached single-car garage that sat far back at the end of the driveway. The two doors were swung open as Carl had taken the car to run an errand. After a couple of trips around the garage I decided the perfect spot to hide was directly behind one of the open doors. I ran to the spot and yanked the door enough to fit behind it. Unfortunately, a pointed steel bar used for chopping ice sat propped up in that very corner. All I remember was a flash of light and then I was looking up at the sky while lying on my back in the snow. I got up, saw the steel rod on the ground, picked it up, and put it back in its original resting place.

We played for another hour or so until my father was back to pick us up. Once back inside the house I removed my hat and felt the back of my head. In the warmth of the kitchen it felt sore and painful. When I took my hand back down there was blood on my fingers. Also, the inside of my hat had a round spot about three inches in diameter. Gertrude and Dad looked at it and decided that I may need to see a doctor.

We piled in the car with Dad and drove back home. Mom looked it over and washed around it. She made a telephone call to Doctor Renaud who lived a few blocks away. His office was attached to his home and Dad took me there immediately.

Being the first time I ever had to go to a doctor, I was nervous. I had been a patient of Doctor Renaud's before, but I don't remember him delivering me. He sat me on a big black table. He applied a local anesthetic to the area and began trimming my hair. It felt somewhat strange while he laced the opening with two stitches. After wrapping my head with a seemingly endless supply of gauze and tape, we were on our way back home.

The last thing I remember when going to bed that night was to sleep on my side and, yes, the Third Grade Curse.

Late in the afternoon on the day following my head injury we were visiting our Aunt Lizzie Greenfield. While there. Aunt Lizzie's telephone rang. She answered the call and passed it on to Dad. The call was from someone in the tool room at Easy Washer where Dad worked. It seemed that one of the large punch press operators was having a problem with a die not properly piercing sheet metal parts. Dad was asked to stop in and take a look at the situation.

Dad invited me to go along with him. When we arrived he met with the guard on duty at the entrance and asked if he could take me in. The guard agreed but stipulated he was to keep me well away from all the machines.

This was my first adventure into a machine shop and factory. While Dad was looking into the problem at hand a good friend of his named Joe asked me what happened to my head. I explained to him the event of the previous day.

Being the type of jovial and outgoing person that Joe was, today we would surely label him as a character. He took my wool cap and wanted me to follow him. He traveled throughout the shop showing everyone we ran into my bloodstained cap and banged head while reciting: "Look what Overend did to his kid so I taking up a collection for the young lad."

Pennies, nickels, dimes, and even a few quarters soon filled the bottom of the inverted cap. When finished, he handed me the cap, laughed loudly, and sent me off to show the "old man" as he put it. Joe sure had a lot of fun teasing Dad that evening.

As for me, I went home with almost two dollars in loose change. That was more money than I had ever seen at that time in my life. Mom made sure I divided it up with my sister and put it in our piggy banks for safe keeping.

Spring finally arrived and my sister was studying to receive her First Holy Communion that coming May. Easter was a short while away and Mom decided to make my sister a new dress. Mom was having a problem with a particular pattern so Gertrude (Trudy)

Reimold came to our house to help her. She brought her youngest daughter Lynda with her and carried her in from the car.

After spending some time, the pattern was conquered and the dress completed. Trudy picked up Lynda and walked down our front steps toward her car. I was playing on the walkway in our driveway when my mother suddenly yelled for me to quickly come out front. When rounding the corner I could not believe what i saw. The manhole cover over the storm drain along side the curb was tilted open and Trudy had fallen into the opening up to her waist. She was holding Lynda in her arms.

Mom screamed for me to go get Lynda and hold her. Lynda was only about a year old but Trudy had managed to set her on the car seat. Mom came over and helped Trudy out of the manhole and into her car. She was fortunate to have escaped with only a large bruise on her hip for several weeks.

We placed the manhole cover back in place and Mom immediately contacted the Syracuse Public Works Department. Workers arrived and welded two support bars across the top of the manhole cover to prevent it from tipping again.

The Reimold's remained good friends of ours through the years. That near-tragic day always remains fresh in my mind and I can't help but attach it to the Third Grade Curse.

Third Grade seemed like nine months of turmoil in my young life. I am sure there were good moments along with the trying ones. As the summer approached, our final school examinations went without a hitch. I made it through the Curse and passed Third Grade. That next fall I would be moving to the large school building and entering the Fourth Grade. The sooner the better as far as I was concerned.

MAKING ENDS MEET

During the late 1940s and early 1950s there was still an atmosphere of recovery from the financial sacrifices made during World War II. Although rationing of food and other necessities was discontinued, much of the population had developed a propensity to be frugal with regard to their management of personal finances. Mom and Dad were very careful with their money and brought us up to follow in their footsteps.

We were not a rich family by any standard. Mom and Dad looked at monetary expenditures with a cautious eye. They provided us with good practical meals and adequate clothing without unnecessary embellishments.

A small closet sat adjacent to the kitchen doorway just off to the side of the sitting room in our Steuben Street home. This closet held the winter coats and clothing for the four of us. Since most of our winter wear was made of wool, the stench of moth balls was ever present within the closet walls. Since Mom and Dad's bedroom only allowed enough room for Mom's dresser, Dad's chest of drawers stood against the opposite wall within the closet. A large business-size envelope was tucked down the left side within the middle drawer. This envelope contained the weekly pay that Dad brought home along with Mom's part-time pay from working at the hospital. All finances were organized around this envelope containing whatever money was available in those moments.

On many occasions Mom and Dad could be heard discussing measures necessary to make ends meet. Being young children, my sister and I never grasped the household money matters. I was always pleased with the bounty we had and never realized at that time how difficult it was for Mom and Dad to maintain a frugal lifestyle.

One of the big events that took place at the Overend household on Steuben Street was justifying the purchase of a deep freezer. Mom and Dad began looking into the value of having a chest freezer in order to purchase meat and other items on sale and be able to store them properly for future consumption. Dad spent significant time at the kitchen table with pencil and paper calculating the practicality of such an investment and anticipated savings along with it. Once they were both convinced, the search for a new freezer started.

Dad picked out a 16 cubic foot General Electric chest freezer and brought it home strapped inside a wooden box he had previously built for hauling items on his boat trailer. The logical location turned out to be in the cellar between the back coal bin and wooden shelves where our canned goods were stored. It turned out to be a very difficult job getting the freezer into the rear door that accessed the cellar landing. Dad and his friends had to completely remove the top lid and struggle while maneuvering the big white chest down the remaining steps to the basement floor. Once in place the top lid was reinstalled and aligned to assure a proper seal. My parents were ever so thankful that the freezer operated well once it was powered up.

Mom and Dad found the new freezer to live up to their expectations. When ground beef was on sale they would buy enough for several meals and freeze some of it. Likewise, they maintained a sorted collection of Birds Eye frozen vegetables. When yellow beans, green beans, squash, and sweet corn were in season, my sister and I would cut and shuck for a weekend so Mom could blanch and freeze a nice supply for the winter months. Vegetable preparation and freezing officially became an annual ritual in our Steuben Street home.

The food processing chores did not end there. There also was canning season. We would go the the tomato fields at a farm named Hafner's on Taft Road in North Syracuse and pick bushels of tomatoes for canning. I remember scalding, coring, and peeling tomatoes for several days at a time while Mom canned, boiled, and sealed the jars. We all liked tomatoes so she would do sixty or seventy quarts of them annually.

Once the tomatoes were canned it was time to make tomato juice. My job was hand cranking the meat grinder that had a juicer attachment. I was always fascinated with putting a tomato in the top of the grinder and collecting the juice in one kettle while all the skins and seeds miraculously emptied into another bucket.

And, it did not end there. I also peeled a lot of pears and peaches that were being canned. In addition, Mom would can her special version of a sweet chili sauce.

Fruitcakes for the Christmas season were next on the list since they had to be baked two months ahead of time and stored for awhile. Mom had her own recipe for that. She did not like the sickening sweetness, as she called it, of currents so she did not use them. Her fruit cake contained mostly wall nuts, dates, and figs. When sliced and buttered it had the texture of a sweetbread only much tastier. Of course, I was always on tap to cut the dates, nuts, and figs. I loved that job because the best benefit of all was snitching and eating some of each item.

Canning and freezing were tedious jobs. Thanks to Mom and Dad's thrifty practices, we always had healthy and nourishing meals. At the same time we were taught valuable lessons that would help us adequately care for our families later in life.

SUMMER OF '50

Every summer day was an adventure in itself. A few of my friends and I had small metal cars and trucks. We would gather at the base of one of the large elm trees that grew on Steuben Street. The roots were large and grew slightly above ground in various arrangements around the base of the tree. The spaces between the roots were filled with dirt that made a great landscape of miniature roads and pathways.

We would use Popsicle sticks to fabricate fences, corrals, and shacks embedded in various locations along our imaginary mountain roads. Reenacting scenes from a recent Gene Autry movie shown at a local movie theater was always serious play. Trucking loose dirt, broken Popsicle sticks, small pebbles, and weed seeds around the root empire seemed to last for hours. Once played out, we would collect our trucks and sticks only to return another day or seek out a different tree for the next episode.

On many occasions throughout the summer you could find yourself without playmates. Household chores took precedence over playtime activity. As it turned out, that was the perfect time to spend with your three-inch diameter red solid-rubber ball.

Rubber balls were readily available at every neighborhood store for a nickel or dime. Having a rubber ball on hand allowed for self-entertainment and exercise.

One of the simplest techniques was standing in one spot on the sidewalk, slamming the ball down in front of yourself, watching it fly skyward, and catching it on the was back down.

Another challenge involved tossing the ball on the roof, letting it roll back down, and catching it as it came back over the edge. Using a slight angle on the toss added mystery as to where along the drip edge the ball would return. If the ball did not return this meant it went over the roof peak, down the other side, and into the neighbor's yard. In that case, it may be as simple as walking to the driveway next door and retrieving it. On rare occasion the outcome could be a bit messier. If per chance it hit the neighbor's house the neighbor might encounter with you in a foul mood. Most always, you would get your ball back. If not, there was always Halloween Day.

Our home had four wooden steps leading up to the front porch. With a little practice, a rubber ball could be tossed at the steps in a slanted downward angle so that it would return as a fly ball. If two were playing, one would stand close to the steps and the other would stand in the street and catch. Fair play involved taking turns at each position.

Since Saint John's was nearby, a walk there with the little red ball could muster up a handball game. Saint John's had a nice handball court on the building wall in the school yard. It seemed like someone was always there to play a game.

One last alternative was DeMong Park. This was a small triangular section of land set aside on the corner of North Salina and Kirkpatrick Streets. A few neighborhood boys, a nice tree branch, and the red rubber ball all contributed to a game of baseball. It was best to bring an old well-worn ball since a good solid hit often resulted in the ball landing in the middle of North Salina Street where it was deemed to be gone forever. At that point the game would end abruptly, especially if it bounced against a passing car. This would be considered an immediate home run. Running the bases was not necessary. We all just ran for home instead. Even back then some drivers could be a bit touchy. As you can see, one ten-cent rubber ball provided a lot of fun and enjoyment.

Another fair-weather friend that could be carried in a pocket was the yo-yo. With nothing else happening during any moment, one would stand on the sidewalk out front of the house and produce a yo-yo. Once spotted by your playmates, they too would show up with their yo-yos. Then the contests would begin.

First everyone would vie to show whose yo-yo could spin the longest time at the end of the string and still be retracted back into their hand. From there the tricks would become more complicated. Around the World was another popular display of talent. The yo-yo was set spinning on the end of the string. Simultaneously, the spinning yo-yo was spun in a three-hundred sixty degree circle after which a full retraction back into one's hand was required.

As I recall, the competition became fierce after awhile. There were complicated sequences like Walk the Dog, Rock the Baby, and Three Leaf Clover. One-by-one we would drop out of the competition. A few kids were naturals at this. I was not, but had a lot of fun trying.

Summer was never all fun and games. Work that needed to be done always seemed to pop up. One such task was getting rid of the tree stump in front of the house where the big elm tree had been removed several years before.

Dad had been noticing that the tree stump had not rotted away as quickly as he had hoped. One day he arrived home from work with a very large electric drill. I helped him run an extension cord from the back room outlet, outside of the house, and down the driveway to the front curb area. Dad positioned the drill directly atop the stump and drilled about twenty deep holes down into the stump.

Once the holes were completed, Dad handed me a bag of rock salt and had me fill each hole to the top. Convinced that the stump would quickly rot, Dad gathered up the drill and returned it to work the next day.

I had not given additional thought to the stump after that day. Later that summer I was standing on the stump and noticed that the salt was gone. It had apparently dissolved into the stump. While kicking around a little I noticed that a chunk broke off one of the edges quite easily.

Being excited about what I had discovered, I ran into the house to let my father know about my discovery. He smiled, it was ready.

He got up, went to the cellar and returned with a roof hatchet. He handed me the hatchet and then told me the job was mine. The stipulations were to take a pail, don't chop while someone is walking by on the sidewalk or a car is drilling by, and make sure all the chips are picked up.

I was surprised. The stump was rotted enough that I devoured it to a hole in the ground, filled the spot with some soil from the garden, and sprinkled grass seed over the area. Mission accomplished, almost anyway.

Sometimes it seemed like these little jobs never ended. The next phase was to fix the cracked and tilted sidewalk that the tree roots had rearranged. This involved carrying out the sawhorses to block the sidewalk from both directions, then breaking the old cement with a sledge hammer and carting it away to be stored for a trip to the dump.

Dad built a form, mixed the cement in a wheelbarrow, and pored a new sidewalk section. When evening came, he hung a kerosene lantern on one sawhorse so anyone traversing the sidewalk could walk around the wet cement.

In all honesty, I found these types of tasks challenging, educational, and very rewarding. This was the summer that I began to realize the feeling of accomplishment in taking on adult tasks. It was not very long before I was mowing the back yard lawn with the old-style reel-type push mower and trimming the front yard with grass shears.

AND THEN, KOREA

It was during the Summer of 1950 that yet one more war had commenced. This war took place in the country of Korea, a small peninsula located in far Southeast Asia only a short distance from Japan.

When World War II had ended in 1945, Korea was divided into two separate entities. As part of the peace agreement, North Korea was to be governed by Russia and South Korea by the United States. The dividing line between the two halves was the thirty-eighth parallel of North latitude.

Unfortunately, the Soviet Communist Regime started crossing the dividing line in an attempt to bring the whole country of Korea under the Communist controlled North. During the years following World War II, many invasions of South Korea were attempted by the North Koreans.

During the summer of 1950, North Korea invaded South Korea. The United Nations Security Council allowed the United States and other countries to provide military support to South Korea. That started a conflict that was to continue for the nest three years.

Recollections of the tough years coping with World War II were on the minds of Steuben Street residents and all United States families. Precautions taken during World War II were to continue in practice throughout the cities in America.

Recycling glass and tin cans remained mandatory. These items were placed in containers and located at the curb periodically for pickup. Tin can preparation was somewhat time consuming. The cans needed to be washed out and the paper labels removed. Both the top and bottom of each can had to be opened, folded down inside the can, then the can flattened on its side. A lot of items came in cans those days and there were no electric can openers available for home use yet.

Air raid drills were also conducted periodically, mostly in the evening after dark. When the city air raid sirens would sound, each family was expected to go inside their house, turn off all lights, and pull down all the shades. Each city block had a Block Captain who would walk up and down the street to check for compliance. If need be, he would knock on a door to politely let someone know if a light was showing outside. It was an eerie sensation since all the street lights in the city were also extinguished at the sound of the siren.

Paper cards with silhouettes of various types of aircraft were printed and distributed. These were used to help observers to quickly identify any aircraft the may fly over as friend or foe.

During the school years that followed 1950, we practiced both fire and air-raid drills. Fire drills taught us how to leave the building promptly, quietly, and safely. Air-raid drills, on the other hand, required us to leave the classroom, sit on the hallway floor in pre-assigned locations, pull our knees up, place our hands over our heads, and wait for a uneventful all-clear signal.

The war years brought heavy tears to some families and miracles to others. I believe Dad's side of the family had encountered some of both. His younger brothers Tom and Joe served in the US Army and survived the ramifications of World War II.

Dad's half-brother Henry had joined the US Army Air Corps and became a tail-gunner on a bomber. While on a mission his aircraft came under attack. He was firing his machine gum at the rear of the aircraft when suddenly the gun stopped firing. He tried clearing it but quickly determined that was not the problem. Not finding anything else wrong, he leaned over sideways to check the ammo belt. He found the belt to be free and not caught on anything.

While he was bent over, an enemy aircraft fired a string of bullets into the tail section of his aircraft. The bullets flung past his arm and body ripping holes through his seat back. He immediately sat back up and found his thumb was gone. One of the bullets had sheared it off.

As suddenly as it had stopped, his machine gun began working again. He had no idea as to why it quit and never found anything wrong with it after that mission. Personally, I would classify that as a miracle of sorts.

Dad had a cousin Robert Shepherd who grew up in Clark Mills, New York. Shortly after the end of World War II, Robert graduated from high school and enlisted in the US Army. After spending almost two years in Japan, his enlistment ended and he safely returned to Clark Mills and restarted his civilian life.

When the Korean conflict erupted in July of 1950, Robert reenlisted into the Army and was assigned to a fighting unit in Korea. Two months into this assignment Robert scaled a hill that needed to be taken and secured. Part way up the hill he was shot by a North-Korea sniper. The large caliber bullet entered his right shoulder, continued through his lung, and embedded itself into his spinal column. He remembered lying on the ground and also losing his vision.

A South-Korean soldier rescued him and rounded up fellow South- Koreans to carry him back down the hill. After several days Robert began regaining his vision. Robert's body, however, was completely paralyzed from the waist down.

Robert was taken to Japan initially and then flown back to the United States for treatment. After several months of surgeries and therapy, he returned home permanently wheelchair bound. From time to time he would reenter the hospital and have loose fragments removed. Because of embedded pieces in critical locations, the bullet was never completely removed.

I remember seeing Robert many times at family functions. He was a cheerful man with a great attitude towards everything.

The Korean war ended in 1953. Like all wars it had taken its toll. Many wartime restrictions were beginning to fade away. America was adjusting itself to get back on track in a new peacetime environment.

FOURTH GRADE

September seemed to be coming faster each year. Before I knew it, school was starting again. The Third Grade Curse was ever fresh in my mind as I headed out to Saint John's to start Fourth Grade.

The Fourth Grade classroom was located on the first floor of the larger school building that faced directly toward Park Street. I entered through the first pair of doors, walked up a short flight of stairs, and entered the classroom directly across the hall at the top of the stairway.

Although the classroom looked much the same, the desks were slightly larger. My new teacher stood at the front of the room directing each of us to our assigned seats.

As I passed in front of her she looked directly into my eyes and smiled. Once seated, she introduced herself as Sister Helen Francis. She was slender and tall. Her voice was quiet and pleasant sounding. I knew right away that there would be no curse that year at school.

In addition to our regular subjects like religion, reading, writing, spelling, and english, we were introduced to geography. I enjoyed this new subject completely. Drawing maps became the highlight of Fourth Grade for me.

Initially, we started with learning the outline of New York State including Long Island. Once grasped, we moved on to adding major cities, lakes, mountains, valleys, and rivers. We were introduced to the location and significance of the Erie Canal. Some of our studies extended to include the early American Indian tribes who resided in New York State and Onondaga County. One of our homework assignments was to construct a layout of an Indian village and bring it to class. This was a classic assignment as far as I was concerned. I not only laid out a village but constructed teepees, firewood from matchsticks, paper canoes, small bows and arrows, also wooden racks for drying fish.

Sister Helen Francis seemed to congratulate me on every assignment I produced. Fourth Grade was turning out to be a good year at school.

It seemed only natural that the map skills I was learning in school should be put to use. This turned out to be the appropriate time to make treasure maps.

First, I needed to have treasure to bury. A quick check of inventory resulted in a small metal car without paint or wheels, a couple of chipped marbles, and a tiny plastic airplane with a broken tail.

Once treasure was identified, locations were carefully chosen in the back yard and each item was buried at least six inches deep.

Small twigs were placed in the ground at each location. Measurements were made and referenced to landmarks such as a specific clothes pole, fence post, sidewalk, or house feature.

When the mapping process was completed the twigs were removed and the treasure was there for future generations to discover.

What became of the treasure is unknown to this day. Maps that were precious at that time would eventually become discarded. Locations were all but forgotten. Some landmarks would have been removed, relocated, or torn down. The Steuben Street treasure may now be lost forever.

One of my father's favorite magazines was the Farm Journal. Before moving to Steuben Street he enjoyed growing vegetables and raising chickens.

Now that we lived in the city and had a chest freezer Dad decided it was time to raise chickens again. Raising them was not very difficult and they would provide a healthy supply of meat during the winter months.

When Spring came, Dad built a small chicken coop in the far corner of the back yard. It was constructed with a wood floor, two-by-four studded walls, and a sloped roof. Stakes were driven into the ground to form an outdoor area. The fencing was two-inch chicken wire all around and over the top also. A small sliding board provided a door that remained open during daylight hours so the chickens could enter and exit via a small walkway called a chicken walk.

One Spring day we arrived home from school for lunch. Mom took us up the back room stairway to the attic. The baby chicks had arrived and Dad had set up a brooder in the back end of the attic area.

The brooder consisted of a four-sided rectangular-shaped wire frame surrounded on all sides with a cloth drape. Over the center area sat a metal shroud that held a light bulb that remained turned on. The chicks roamed free in this heated area and congregated under the warmth of the light bulb.

Occasionally, we would check on them and shoo any escapees back into the brooder. The brooder also contained a trough for feed and a metal chicken waterer.

Dad would purchase his baby chicks by mail order from Montgomery Wards Co. The chicks were shipped in a cardboard box that had half-inch diameter holes around the outside. When the chicks arrived we could hear them peeping inside the box since it contained about fifty chicks. Mom would take the box up to the attic, open it, and place the chicks one-by-one into the brooder. My sister and I always got to hold one of the fuzzy little birds.

The chicks would grow fast, doubling their size in a week or so. It was not long before they were placed outside in the chicken coop. Once out there the chickens needed to be powdered for lice on occasion.

Dad never had any problems changing the water and adding cracked corn to the feeders. It was entertaining to watch Mom do the same. The chickens did not take to her so well. They would gang up on her and peck at her ankles anytime she entered the coop. Dad always had a lot of fun passing that one around. My sister and I were not allowed to spend time in the chicken coop, mainly because chickens could be nasty sometimes.

In total, we had fifty chickens in the coop that Spring and Summer. They would go inside and outside, eating, sleeping, and drinking at their leisure. This would continue until Fall arrived.

During the last few months of the school year the weather began to warm quite nicely. Mom worked either days or evenings on Saturdays at the hospital. After some coaxing from time to time, Dad would shuttle us around in the car for some excitement.

Since I began studying about local explorers and the various Indian tribes, one of my favorite trips was to the French Fort on Onondaga Lake Parkway. We would park in the small parking lot and walk up a somewhat overgrown pathway to the fort entrance. After signing in we would visit the various buildings like the blacksmith shop, soldier quarters, baking kitchen, and chapel.

One large building housed a real birch-bark canoe, some bear furs, and a actual American Indian ceremonial beaded outfit. Since it was traditional, we always tossed a penny into the canoe.

Before leaving the fort we would climb the log ladders to elevated platforms where sentries once stood when defending the fort. On occasion, we would pretend reenacting a battle or two.

Prior to returning to the car, there was one last thing we needed to do. The fort sat on high ground with a grassy slope about twenty feet up from the parking lot level. The final thrill consisted of lying flat on the ground and rolling log-style down the grassy slope to the bottom. This sweeping exit did not seem to bother Dad. However, Mom's annoyance over the grass stains on our clothing could be heard echoing the remainder of the weekend.

Another favorite Saturday pastime was visiting the Burnet Park Zoo. Back in the year 1951 the zoo was not nearly the size it is today. One main building existed with a large center aisle and cages lining both sides. Each cage had a heavy metal door that was opened on fair-weather days to allow the animals access to the outside air. A few larger animals roamed about outside in separate corrals.

A pathway led past two outdoor cages containing foxes that hardly ever showed themselves. Continuing on the pathway, the next area of interest was a duck pond. We loved stopping there to feed popcorn to the ducks. Watching them squabble over a handful of corn always caused us to laugh.

The pathway ended at a stone building that housed bears. They spent the majority of the cold-weather days sleeping. Even though the zoo was small by today's standards, to us it was enjoyable on every visit.

On other Saturdays we were drawn to visit the Salt Museum located in Liverpool, New York. This museum contained many artifacts associated with the salt industry so prevalent throughout the Town of Salina in the years gone by.

The museum contained many photos of the Galeville and Liverpool areas relating to the salt brine pumping and processing era. On many occasions we stood and watched an older man make baskets from willow shoots that were harvested in the area.

My mother told us of how she and her siblings would harvest willow shoots along the creek bank as a child. They were paid a penny for each bundle of these shoots when taken to a local basket maker. Once in awhile they were hired to strip the bark skin from the shoots that had been soaked in water. Again, a lot of work for a penny or two.

Upon leaving the museum, Dad would walk with us along the shore of Onondaga Lake to a local yacht club. My sister and I would walk out on each dock and view the fancy yachts close-up. We marveled at the size and structure of these wooden boats.

Looking down into the water we would watch large carp swimming about in the shade of the boats. They moved slowly and seemed to spend a lot of time scouring the stone shoreline wall for morsels of food.

Back in the classroom, these Saturday excursions provided me with insight into much of what our studies were all about. Summer was once again on its way. School exams were approaching rapidly. Attending school this year was truly an enjoyable and pleasant experience.

SUMMER OF '51

At any rate, the Summer season appeared just as it always had. Male cicadas generated their loud shrill raspy sounds from the treetops throughout the Syracuse north side. Steuben Street had its share of these perpetual noise makers.

Each day brought new adventure. We used our brains and whatever resources we could locate to make many of our play items. In almost all cases designing an item, sketching a plan, locating materials, and constructing the finished toy-of-the-day took a lot of time. Most of the pleasure resulted from this process rather than just playing with a store-bought toy.

Early Summer days tended to be breezy, just right for kite flying. Purchasing a kite and a roll of string would have been a quick solution. However, the total cost of these store-bought items would come close to thirty-five cents or a little more.

Store-bought was not an option. Finding a couple of bottles to trade for some penny candy was one thing. Thirty-five cents back then was unheard of for children to amass.

The first thing we needed to do was walk to the corner stores and locate an old orange crate. The next step was to ask the store owner for the crate. Sometimes, you may need to help the storekeeper carry in some items to earn a crate.

After arriving back home with the crate, it needed to be disassembled. This was generally accomplished using a pocket knife and small hammer. Once the noise started my mother would always make an appearance from nowhere and quickly point out that I was junk-picking again and dragging garbage back home. A brilliant performance was then rendered to convenience her that this was treasure and not junk. The tone would then change to: "Make sure you clean up the mess when you're done before your father gets home from work."

Continuing on, the pocket knife was used to slit the crate side panels into thin sticks. Wrapping string and applying white glue would result in longer lengths of wood. These slit pieces were then arranged into a cross formation and held in place using more string and white glue. String and glue were used yet again to form the outside edge of string that went from tip to tip around the kite frame.

Paper was easy to come by. Newspaper was the covering of choice. If the wind was too much for newspaper to tolerate, a quick trip to Cavelli's Meat Market just around the corner on Pond Street resulted in a few feet of meat wrapping paper for free.

Once the kite was done and the glue dried, a cloth strip was needed for a tail to stabilize it in flight. If Mom did not have anything she considered old enough to contribute, a quiet trip down the cellar stairs would certainly yield an old rag that Dad had left lying around.

One last trip a couple of blocks down Park Street to Myers Market generally yielded enough string to fly the kite.

Kites were tested in the back yard away from the maze of power lines that lined Steuben Street. Once proven worthy to fly, a trip to the school yard or DeMong park provided ample space for flight.

Stepping back for a minute, one may wonder why the meat markets would have wrapping paper and string. Back in this era there were no plastic food plates or plastic wrap. All meats were displayed in glass enclosed refrigeration units with slanted windows on the front for customer viewing and selection.

Customers would select what they wanted. Hamburg was ground by the butcher at the time of purchase. Steaks and chops were also prepared when a purchase was being made.

Three items sat on the large counter, a scale, roll of paper, and string dispenser. The meat being purchased was weighed on the scale and the cost was calculated by hand with pencil and paper. When acceptable to the buyer, a large sheet of brown paper was pulled from the roll and cut off with a knife bar that sat against the roll itself. The paper was then placed flat on the counter and the meat wrapped within. String was then dispensed, wrapped around the paper bundle several times, tied in a knot and snapped off to be left hanging ready for the next order.

This was the Summer that Mom and Dad decided to re-wallpaper the parlor and sitting room walls. Initially, the furniture and rug was removed from the parlor as that was the room chosen to finish first.

The parlor walls were constructed of wood lath and covered with a plaster mix. Since our Steuben Street home was built around the year 1900, drywall had not yet been invented.

Each wall in the parlor had four layers of wallpaper already built up on them. The decision was made to remove all four layers down to the bare plaster wall. Mom started on one wall, soaking the various layers with a sponge soaked in water. Using a small putty knife she would skillfully remove several layers at a time.

Seeing me watching her with fascination, she offered me the sponge and putty knife so I could try. I think that became the mackerel the caught the tuna. The next thing I realized was my promotion to a master wallpaper- remover position. My new summertime chore was now official.

Things moved right along. I found areas where the bottom layer of paper was no longer attached to the plaster so it fell off easily with very little soaking. Being curious about what some of the underlying layers looked like, I started to remove one layer at a time. That is, until I got caught and had to be reminded that Mom wanted the job done sooner rather than later.

Mom would help if she had time available. I did most of the removal myself and really enjoyed the accomplishment. Dad was really pleased that the plaster was gouged very little when I had finished.

I did not participate in hanging the new wallpaper. This obviously required skills that I was not yet old enough to grasp. Uncle Johnny Greenfield came over, brought his wallpaper preparation table and cutter, and helped Mom and Dad do the papering. The room looked very cozy once finished. Mom truly had good taste in selecting wallpaper designs and colors.

Since the parlor was now complete, the next step was moving the rug and furniture back in. Next, the whole effort was again repeated in the sitting room. The walls there had far fewer layers of old paper to remove. It went a lot smoother.

One toy we played with a lot in the neighborhood was a cap gun. Many times we staged western movie scenes by running to and fro on the sidewalks of Steuben Street. Hiding from tree to tree we would act out shootouts using our cap guns.

The caps were long strips of paper containing evenly spaced blisters of some sort of gunpowder that would make a popping sound when struck by the metal hammer of a cap pistol. The paper cap rolls had small holes spaced between each powder blister so they could ratchet into position inside the cap gun each time the trigger was pulled.

On one fine day the corner store put a new toy on display that took the neighborhood by surprise almost overnight. It was a plastic bomb-shaped toy about three inches in length. The front end had a molded cap containing a floating metal stud. This cap could be unscrewed to allow insertion of an individual cap. The opposite end had four fins. Once loaded with a cap, the plastic bomb was tossed up into the air. It would then drop vertically to a hard surface giving off a loud popping sound as the nose pin struck the sidewalk.

The lazy silence of summer was disrupted many days since both boys and girls enjoyed the cap bombs. One day I decided to try obtaining a louder sound from the little plastic bomb. I peeled two caps from a roll, carefully aligned the powder blisters directly over each other, and loaded them into the nose cavity of the bomb. I then tossed it high into the air and watched it land with a noise louder that a simple pop. This soon caught on with most of the bomb-tossers on the street.

For me, this just was not enough to satisfy my insatiable curiosity. I had to extend my personal experiment to three caps at one time. I secluded myself at the back porch steps and loaded the bomb. I tossed it high in the air but nothing happened when it landed on the back sidewalk. Being curious, I retrieved the bomb, held it high in the air, swung hard, and flung the bomb nose down onto the sidewalk. The three caps went off simultaneously with a very loud bang. At the same time, the mini-explosion blew the cap off the end of the bomb.

Within seconds Mom was out the back door investigating the noise. I carefully explained that a cap had made the sound. She bought the story and advised me to move farther from the screen door when making noise. That's exactly what I did.

My adventures with caps did not end that day. I subsequently wiped out a cap gun using multiple-caps in it. Another time when Mom was at work I used a hammer to hit eight or nine caps at the same time. Now, that was noise. Experimentation with caps ended the day I decided to hit a whole roll with a hammer. The noise was deafening and the hammer flew out of my hand.

The show was over. I had reached the point of satisfaction. Dad came out the back door just as I slid the hammer out of sight. He found me sitting on the back step holding my cap gun. He asked me not to shoot anymore caps for awhile because I was disturbing the neighborhood too much. I nodded. After he went back inside I retrieved the hammer, put it away, and went off seeking adventure doing something else.

The time had arrived to put my Fourth Grade education to work. I pocketed my jackknife, then headed out front and down Steuben Street. Around the corner and up Pond Street was the Hilltop Laundry. Along side the laundry was an overgrown area of small and medium sized trees.

Within minutes I had selected and cut a five-foot long branch that looked ideal for forming a bow. Arriving back home, I sat on the back step, trimmed up the sides of the branch, and cut notches radially around each end.

Knowing just where some heavy string sat, I quietly navigated to the cellar and loped off a six-foot piece. I pocketed the string and made my way back outside. I attached the string to both ends of the branch, tightening it with enough tension to form a suitable bow.

The next step involved slitting leftover side panels from a fruit crate and whittling them into a smooth shape for arrows. Setting up a cardboard box and hand-drawn target by the chicken coop door resulted in a nice archery range.

Many summer days on Steuben Street were filled with warm sunshine, but we had our share of rainy days as well. One of my favorite pastimes on a rainy day was playing the phonograph. The phonograph we had was hand-cranked record player fitted inside a large wooden cabinet. The records were about ten inches in diameter and ran at a speed of seventy-eight revolutions per minute. To operate the phonograph, a threaded crank was removed from it's storage place in the cabinet and inserted into a round opening in the side of the cabinet. The crank was then turned clockwise until the threads bottomed and the motor spring could be wound. Winding the crank generally took about thirteen or fourteen complete rotations. The phonograph had to be hand cranked each time a record was to be played.

No electricity was used. The turntable was rotated by a motor run with the mechanical spring. A tone arm was a tapered hollow metal tube extended from a location near the back corner of the phonograph. Attached to the end of the tone arm was a device called a reproducer. The reproducer contained a replaceable needle that was manually placed on each record to start it playing music. The reproducer would take vibrations from the record grooves, vibrate a diaphragm within itself, and generate air motions within the tone arm producing sounds prerecorded on the record.

On our phonograph, the tone arm was connected to a large wooden speaker that flared open at the front allowing buildup of sound volume into the room. I would pull out a stack of records that Mom and Dad had from the 1930s and play them for hours. My goal was to play every song on both sides of every record they had. Unfortunately, that goal was never reached in one setting. Either I grew tired after awhile or was eventually interrupted to apply my energy to chores that needed doing.

Once the sun was back out, the old phonograph sat idle waiting in the corner for another rainy summer day.

Every Saturday was bath day unless we got into something that required a complete dunk sooner. Generally, we made it to Saturdays.

Hot water heaters back then were not automatic. Our heater was connected to the natural gas line. To get hot water from a faucet we would need to get stick matches, go down cellar, get on our hands and knees, manually open a gas valve under the hot water tank, and light the burner that sat out in the open directly beneath the tank itself.

Once lit, the tank had to be checked often to monitor the water temperature with the flat of hand to assure the tank was not overheating. When the tank was hot about three-quarters of the way to the top, the gas had to be turned off. Turning off the tank was one thing you never ever wanted to forget to do as it would end up overheating and exploding.

Our bathtub was a large cast-iron porcelain coated claw foot tub. Each time one bath was complete, the hot water heater ritual would again need to be accomplished.

One bath a week did not mean that I was home free for the next seven days. Each evening washing was done at the kitchen sink. The water was heated in a large kettle on the kitchen stove.

The kitchen sink was quite large and hung on the wall that faced the back room. Again, it was cast iron with a porcelain finish. The left half of the sink was a convoluted drain board while the right half was the sink itself. A small metal pan sat beneath the sink and we used it for washing.

I remember that I would brush my teeth, wash my hair, and bathe completely using this basin in the kitchen sink.

Once in awhile my mother and father needed to go shopping at the market or shopping without us children. On one such occasion a friend of Mom's came to the house to watch us for a couple of hours. Her name was Rita.

Rita was a petite lady and spoke with a very soft voice. She arrived on time then Mom and Dad left in the car. My parents were barely down the street when Rita picked up her magazine, a box of Fanny Farmer candy, and stretched out on top of my bed.

My sister and I were playing at the kitchen table for awhile, then went to the bedroom doorway to find Rita reading and eating candy. Naturally, we asked for a piece of candy. Rita refused. So, we decided to make a little mischief for ourselves.

Upon going back into the kitchen, we got into the bag of ground coffee, took some outside, and proceeded to mix in with water in a tin can. Since it did not dissolve in cold water, we were left with only a can of wet ground coffee beans. We dumped most of it in the driveway and rinsed the can under the outside faucet.

Looking for something better to mix, we drifted down cellar where we spotted a bag of concrete cement and some canning jars. Figuring this would be great for making stone molded items, we quickly filled a couple of jars with concrete and headed back outside.

We mixed some of the concrete with water and tried to seal some of the separations between sections of the back yard sidewalk thinking this would improve the surface for roller skating. The mix turned out to be too watery and only left a mess.

I had one big jar left to mix, so I did. I poured some out figuring to make a stone figure but quickly realized that soupy concrete could not be hand formed into anything useful.

Then it happened. Without warning Mom and Dad were back. I hurriedly hid the jar I had around the corner of the chicken coop. Mom immediately spotted the coffee grounds and the cement on the sidewalk. She was only starting to respond when she found the kitchen in disarray with spilled coffee on the floor and table.

She instantly asked where Rita was. I proudly responded: "On my bed eating a box of candy and reading a book."

Two days later things were beginning to calm down again when Dad walked into the house with a large canning jar filled with hardened cement. He was angry and insisted on knowing if there were any more hidden around. Of course, the answer was no.

A secondary flare-up existed for a couple of more days. Things finally quieted down after that.

Funny thing, Rita was never again asked to watch us. Would a piece of candy prevented all this turmoil? Who knows, maybe, maybe not.

Many of our neighbors on Steuben Street felt that my sister and I were well brought-up children. I have to agree with that, although, the jury is still out on whether or not Mom felt the same way. You see, on rare occasion, we were tempted to and indulged in a bout of minor rowdiness.

One such episode involved a neighbor that displayed a nasty disposition much of the time. This particular neighbor had a nasty habit of trying to boss my sister and I around while we played peacefully within the confines of our own backyard. One warm summer day he pressed our buttons once too often.

This particular neighbor had a large orange cat that he babied like a princess. After bossing us around a bit, he put the cat down and reentered his house. After a short wait, my sister and I snuck over the fence, into his back yard, picked up the cat and hid it in an old wooden icebox that sat near his porch. After returning to our own yard we sat and waited for the next blast of sass.

Within about fifteen minutes, we were off on other adventures and forgot about the cat. About a half-hour had elapsed when we returned to the backyard again. We both gulped upon hearing the neighbor outside calling his cat by name. All of a sudden, in a sweet voice, he politely asked us if we saw his cat. Naturally, we told him no.

Realizing that this situation was now becoming desperate, it was time to save the day and the cat too. I stepped up and reported to him that some kids I did not know were in his yard playing with the cat and they were also opening and closing the old icebox. He immediately went over to the icebox, opened the door and retrieved his cat. The cat looked a little winded but turned out to be just fine. As he walked up the steps of his side porch, he stopped, turned around and recited the line we had heard so many times in the past: "If I find you two did this, I'm a gonna tell-a you momma."

In modern day terminology, I guess you would conclude that we dodged a bullet.

It was one week before school was to begin again when Mom and Dad announced that we would be going to the New York State Fair. I was excited.

Back then the State Fair was more about farming, growing vegetables and flowers, raising animals, seeing new gadgets, and the latest farm machinery. Normally, Mom would pack some sandwiches for lunch. This year, however, Grandma Brown's Beans was offering baked bean sandwiches for a nickel each. This was deemed a large enough bargain so carrying a lunch would not be necessary.

My interests were always best served by a trip through the Center of Progress Building. I would amass a collection of pamphlets, brochures, booklets, and catalogs beyond belief. Mostly all of it pertained to raising farm animals, poultry, and growing various vegetables. These items would occupy my reading list for weeks after the fair ended.

Many new kitchen products were displayed and demonstrated. Although my parents liked browsing these items, I only recall Mom ever purchasing one such gadget, a round cast metal grilled cheese sandwich maker.

Although she used this implement on occasion to make us grilled cheese sandwich pies, she always complained about the waste of trimming the crust off the bread. In our home, nothing ever went to waste. The crust trimmings were always saved and mixed with hamburg the next day for hamburg patties.

Our visit to the State Fair was always an educational experience. There was no room in the family budget for money to waste on midway rides or games of chance. We never cared because there was plenty of other things to see and do.

Several different buildings were used for housing the animals on display. There was one for cows, another for chickens and ducks, and yet more for hogs, goats, sheep, and horses. It truly was a treat to tour them all.

We left the fairgrounds for home late in the afternoon, all tired and a bit weary. Once back home I would sort my paperwork collection and categorize it for future reading.

The State Fair always ended on Labor Day weekend. This was the childhood signal that school would be back in session the Wednesday after Labor Day. Time was now spent checking to make sure our school clothes were in order. If shirts were outgrown, new ones were bought, washed, dried, and starched if necessary. A new pair of shoes always accompanied the start of school. We had to wear them around the house over Labor Day weekend to break them in.

One additional trip to the lot in Brewerton was made to load the boat onto the trailer and bring it into the backyard for winter storage.

Celebrating Elaine's eighth birthday in the Steuben Street kitchen (1951).

Our Christmas tree in the sitting room in 1951.

FIFTH GRADE

The first day back at school each Fall always seemed a bit stressful. For one thing, we never knew who our teacher would be. This particular year my teacher's name was Sister Agnella.

Sister Agnella was much older than the teachers I had had during previous years. She also impressed me as being a bit on the stern side, very seldom cracking a smile.

As I moved up in grade at school, I began to put more emphasis on events that took place outside rather than those in the classroom. It's not that I was not interested in my school work, the school work just seemed to become more routine and maybe less adventurous. Much of what I recall of Fifth Grade occurred beyond the school walls.

Early in the school term we were visited in the classroom by a representative from the Syracuse Savings Bank. The presentation he gave related to the benefits of setting up and maintaining a savings account. I took the cards he provided home and had my parents help me fill them out. Mom thought this was a good idea.

Every two weeks after that visit the banker would show up at school, accept deposits, and make appropriate entries into our bank savings books. With each visit I would deposit fifty cents. Since the interest rate was one- percent annually, it seemed very slow growing.

Upon arriving home one Friday afternoon that Fall, Mom had us change our clothes quickly. It turned out that this was to be the weekend that we would process the chickens. Dad had already begun lopping their heads off and dunking them in hot water to kill off any lice and get the feathers to stand up a bit.

My task for this whole weekend was pulling feathers from the chickens being processed, making sure to remove all the tiny pin feathers also. In- between time, Dad would remove the giblets and carve the separate pieces. Mom would then wash everything really well, wrap each chicken in freezer paper, mark the date on the outside, and store them in the chest freezer.

This allowed us to have baked chicken each Sunday for dinner year round. The dinner was always accompanied with baked potatoes and a vegetable.

Like many other items, butter was rationed during the war years. My parents would purchase a substitute spread called margarine. My sister and I both grew up using margarine on our toast and sandwiches.

When margarine was first supplied to the public it was white and not yellow like butter. Many people avoided margarine because of the color. Eventually, margarine was packaged as one-pound units in a plastic bag. As I recall, the bag was about three inches wide by nine inches long and contained a small membrane on the inside wall that held a yellow dye.

Many times I sat at the kitchen table and watched Dad squeeze the package of margarine to soften it. Then he would pinch the side of the bag to release the yellow dye into the margarine. It would take him about twenty minutes to completely massage the dye throughout the margarine until it transformed the color to that of butter.

My sister and I grew up on margarine and we always called it butter. Dad always laughed about the time he treated us to a stick of real butter and we hated it. To this day I still prefer margarine over butter.

As school days inched their way toward Thanksgiving vacation, I began feeling the urge to bring up my desire to play the accordion. Mom seemed somewhat warmed a bit toward the idea but constantly reminded me that I would need to practice my music lessons daily. Sometimes it seemed close, then other times it drifted out of the picture.

Presenting the idea turned out to be easier than I thought. There was one question Mom always asked us around Thanksgiving time. She would inquire as to what one gift we would like Santa to bring that year, making sure we understood not to be selfish. After much thought, I decided the best way to assure success was to call on a power higher than Mom and Dad, so that would be none other than Santa Claus. Yes, my Christmas list had only one item on it that year and it was an accordion. The campaign was officially launched on that Thanksgiving weekend.

Just after Thanksgiving each year the Easy Washing Machine Company would have their annual Family Christmas Party. This was always held at the Syracuse War Memorial Auditorium on South State Street in Syracuse. Mom, Dad, my sitter, and I always looked forward to attending.

Since all seating was open to everyone, we would arrive early and selected seats along a cement wall about ten rows up from the main floor. Mom liked this spot best since no people would be sitting directly behind and kicking the seat backs.

The auditorium itself consisted of a large open area that was transformed into an ice-skating rink. Seating flowed around three sides of the arena and a stage stood in the fourth location.

Large American flags hung from staffs mounted high up on each side of the stage. The event always commenced with lights dimming, spotlights trained on the flags, and us standing to sing the National Anthem. Hidden blowers in the wall were run to provide a breeze for the flags to wave in.

Entertainment varied from year to year. Various vocalists were on stage to lead us singing Christmas Carols. Clowns on ice skates roamed the ice rink while performing their antics. Professional ice skaters wearing bright sequenced outfits danced flawlessly around the rink. One year there was a speed skater barrel-jumper that had us holding our breath with each jump. The show always closed with a visit from Santa Claus. He and his elves would hand out candy canes as we gathered along the rail to exit after the festivity.

The grand finale for us kids was the distribution of children's gifts. Each employee was issued a tag with a string on it. This tag was presented to helpers distributing a gift to each girl and boy. The tag each child wore was color coded for the appropriate gift. We could hardly wait to get home and open our gift.

Some of the gifts I remember receiving were modeling clay, a flashlight that looked like a ray gun, and an assortment of plastic Kazoos the looked like small musical instruments.

I am sure my mother relished the day that the last kazoo ever played.

Christmas 1951 had finally arrived. After bounding out of bed my sister and I found gifts neatly sorted around the Christmas tree. Before opening gifts we would wash, dress, and bundle up to walk to church for Christmas Mass.

There was always some snow on the ground. The morning air was fresh and brisk. If it had snowed the day before the ground cover would be pure white. However, fallen snow that stood for a few days always displayed the remnants of black soot distributed across the ground from smokestacks that stood mightily throughout the area.

Saint John's Church was magnificently decorated. There were bows of evergreens with red ribbons distributed throughout. Many beeswax candles provided bright twinkling light around the alter area. Centered on the alter steps directly behind the Communion rail was the manger with the Christ child lying on straw. The hymns sung that morning were all Christmas Carols. Everyone in attendance seemed to be in a joyful mood.

Upon arriving back home we shed our coats, ate breakfast, and headed into the sitting room to open our gifts. My eyes lit up when

I opened the gift that had a sticker from Santa Claus on it. Yes, it was a twelve-base piano- accordion, just what I wanted.

My sister opened her gift and had received a special doll. It had a pink dress, bonnet, and an internal record cartridge. When wound, the doll would recite a bedtime prayer.

Our Christmas tree was a balsam. Dad would always pick one out and purchase it about ten days before Christmas. He would leave it on the back porch standing in a bucket of water to help keep it fresh. About four days before Christmas he would bring it and the bucket into the back room to allow warmth so the branches could settle before decorating. After a couple of more days Dad would cut the tree base, trim a lower branch or two, and mount it in the stand. At that point we would all start decorating.

It turned out that the perfect location for the tree was in the sitting room between the two side windows. Dad always started first since his big task was placing the lights on the tree and adjusting their positions to assure they would not come in contact with the tree branches or needles. Each light was a six- watt bulb that would generate quite a lot of heat. Once Dad had installed and checked all the lights, they would not be relit until Christmas Day itself.

Glass ornaments were next to be hung on the tree. Small ones went toward the top while large ones hung beneath. Each year my sister and I would enjoy looking at the ornaments. We each had our favorites.

Mom would pop popcorn and we would sit for a couple of hours stringing each piece onto long lengths' of thread. When finished, the popcorn was draped from branch to branch on the tree. Finally, foil icicles were placed on the tree. This was very time consuming since many of these icicles were individually hung on each branch.

After the tree was decorated, a winter village scene was set under the tree. A large field of snow was simulated using fluffy cotton cut from rolls. The cotton was placed around the tree stand and spread out on the floor covering a five-foot by five-foot area.

A large printed-paper nativity was assembled and placed directly in front of the tree. Off to the left side towards the back sat a paper doll house that Dad had since he was a small boy. A smaller paper house was positioned toward the right rear side. Directly in front of that was a log cabin that was constructed from a small Lincoln Log set. A small white country church occupied the space between the log cabin and manger. Once in position, all these items were lit inside with a special string of lights that Dad had made.

At this point, the arrangement was turned over to my sister and me. We would open the large box of artifacts that Mom and Dad had collected since childhood and start placing them under the tree. There were farm animals, wire trees, Santa's on skis, penguins, birds, and a wind-up dog that carried a slipper in it's mouth. The dog was a gift from my father to my mother when they were dating in the early 1930s.

A major portion of the remaining items came from Dad's childhood collection of Tootsie Toys. He had small trains, cars, boats, and airplanes that we arranged wherever space permitted.

Track for Dad's electric train was routed around the perimeter of the cotton field. Once the engine and cars were placed on the tracks, a couple of runs were made to assure the train would run properly. A small red and green picket fence surrounded the finished snow field.

One more embellishment was added. A string of bubble lights was clipped on the fence and ran around the outside from wall to wall. When the tree and scene were lit, I was always content to sit and relax while staring at the whole display.

Throughout our childhood years my sister and I would add new items that we received on special occasions throughout the years.

One tradition that Mom always adhered to took place shortly after the Thanksgiving holiday. She would bring out a picture of Santa Claus and hang it on a upper cupboard door in the kitchen. Upon doing so she would remind my sister and me that Santa would be watching our every move between then and Christmas Eve so we had better behave. If we got out of hand on occasion she would clear her throat and point to the picture.

Mom used this right up into and including the latter years of our childhood on Steuben Street. She stressed that it applied to all gifts expected from her and Dad as well as Santa, always threatening that Santa would leave coal in our stockings.

One day Mom was aggravated with my sister and me over something that did not seem to make sense to us. We politely pointed out that Santa was watching her too. She immediately walked over to the picture, smacked it with her hand a couple of times, and made a rude comment about a fat old man with a white beard. We immediately responded by letting her know that Santa was not going to like that.

Well, the days passed and Christmas Eve finally arrived. We hung our stockings on a cardboard fireplace that Dad assembled each year for Christmas. Mom had just hung one of her ankle socks on the hook when I chose to mention how rude she had been to Santa's picture. This immediately started something.

Mom took down her sock and went into the bedroom. A few seconds later she returned with a large full-length nylon stocking. She hung the stocking on the fireplace where it flowed from the mantle and down partially across the floor. She made one quick comment about letting the fat man fill this one and went back into the kitchen laughing.

My sister and I were mortified. We just knew the outcome would not be good. After sleeping soundly all night, we arose and headed into the sitting room. There, on the floor, was her nylon stocking filled to the brim with coal. While our emotions were running high, she was peeking around the doorway laughing. Dad came in laughing and commented that the coal could be used to heat the house. He quickly carried it downstairs and emptied it into the coal bin.

There was a note from Santa on the kitchen table thanking us for the milk and cookies we left for him. He also included a couple of lines that warned Mom to behave and not hit his picture anymore. In addition, he announced that there truly were gifts for her in the closet but she had better behave.

We were amazed that Santa was such a jolly good fellow and took it all in stride. That is, until we figured this all out. Ho. Ho. Ho.

Christmas Days on Steuben Street were always cozy, bright, and fun filled. Mom would prepare a special dinner. After dinner, Christmas cookies and fruit cake were offered for dessert. Around supper time Uncle Johnny and Aunt Marie Greenfield would come to visit. Uncle Johnny's face would light up as we always presented him with White Owl cigars as he was an avid cigar smoker. Aunt Lizzie Greenfield was not far behind. She always made sure each of us children got a small gift from her.

Throughout the week following Christmas we would visit some of our aunts and uncles.

It did not take long for New Year's Eve to arrive. During the wintertime, the trees outside were barren of leaves. We would look out of the back door and see the top of the State Tower building. It was lit with alternating red and green lights that changed about every sixty seconds or so.

At exactly midnight on New Year's Eve, tradition provided for all the church bells in Syracuse to ring out. Mom would have us up and standing at the back door listening. As the hour arrived, one bell in the distance would start pealing, followed by another, and then more, until the whole city was alive with bells. This lasted for five or ten minutes and then the city would fall silent again for another year.

Our Christmas tree was lit all evening on New Year's Day. The following day the boxes were brought out and everything was disassembled to be packed away. Once dismantled, Dad would cut the tree in half and leave both halves in the back yard for us to play with. Eventually, they would be drug to the curb for pickup during mid-January.

My parents did not waste any time getting me started on music lessons. They located an instructor named Irving Metzger who played the accordion at the Pastime Club on North Salina Street. Mr. Metzger lived in Clay, NY but drove to Syracuse and taught accordion to students in their individual homes. My first lesson was in mid-January of 1952.

Back at school a new problem had developed for me. Taking music lessons at home required me to be there at the exact same time that school let out for the day. So, every Tuesday I was expected to get excused from school fifteen minutes early in order to be home when Mr. Metzger arrived.

Mom wrote a note explaining this to my teacher Sister Agnella. Initially, I would get up from my seat, slip on my coat and boots, and quietly leave for the day. Then, the worst began to happen. Sister Agnella decided that I could wait the additional fifteen minutes and dismiss with the rest of the class.

For the remainder of the school year this posed a big problem. Mr. Metzger would arrive at our house. I would raise my hand and report that I needed to leave. Sister Agnella would respond in the negative. A few minutes later my father would be standing at the classroom doorway telling her that I was late for my music lesson. Sister Agnella in turn would tell him that I should raise my hand and let her know.

Sister Agnella was getting up in age. I always struggled with whether she actually forgot or just did not like me. Either way, taking music lessons and traversing Fifth Grade became a perpetual struggle for the remainder of that school year.

It was during the Spring of 1952 on a Saturday evening that a somewhat scary thunderstorm passed over the Syracuse area. There was a lot of lightening flashing and thunder rolling. Eventually, the power went out and all of Steuben Street was in the dark. Dad took his trusty three-cell metal flashlight and headed down the cellar stairs to fetch the kerosene lantern.

My sister and I sat silently in the kitchen darkness until he returned. He placed the lantern in the center of the kitchen table and lit the wick with a match. Once adjusted, the lantern illuminated the room completely.

Dad pulled out a deck of cards and taught us how to play Rummy. After a few hands we caught on and played for over an hour or so. During this time the storm subsided and we waited silently for the power to finally return exactly at out bedtime.

I turned ten years old in April of that year. My friend Johnny convinced me that I should join the Boy Scouts and gave me an application form for my parents to complete. My parents completed the form and I joined up.

My troop was Troop 134 and it was sponsored by Saint John the Baptist Academy where I attended school. Our troop meetings were in the old school auditorium every Monday evening from seven to nine o'clock throughout the school year.

After attending my first scout meeting my mother took me to a store downtown named Dey Brothers. They had an official Boy Scout department where Mom was able to purchase my first uniform, proper colored neckerchief, troop insignia, pocket knife, and Boy Scout Handbook.

When we arrived back home I immediately started studying my handbook. As the next few weeks progressed I managed to memorize and recite the Scout Oath, Law, Slogan, and Motto. In addition, I learned to tie a complete variety of knots, correctly fold the American flag, and learn various other things a new scout needed to know.

The time came when I was tested on my basic scout knowledge and became qualified for the rank of Tenderfoot. I was introduced to the Court of Honor ceremony shortly before school let out for the summer and was awarded my Tenderfoot badge. Mom proudly sewed the badge onto my left shirt pocket.

Summer vacation had arrived. Report cards were handed out in mid- June on schedule. My sister and I had passed all our final examinations and were advanced to our next grades.

A GRAY CLOUD LOOMED

It was on a Saturday afternoon in 1951 when life suddenly tossed a curve in our direction. Dad was parked on Prospect Avenue in front of Saint Joseph's Hospital while we waited for Mom to come out after work. We knew she was a little late but sometime nurses needed to stay a little longer than usual.

At last the hospital door opened and we immediately knew something was wrong. Mom was walking very slowly down the wide walkway and somewhat hunched forward. When she arrived at the car Dad held the door open for her. She had great difficulty getting into the front seat and commented that her legs felt numb.

On the ride home that afternoon she told us what had happened. Mom had lifted a patient on her own and felt a pain in her back. Later, as she retrieved her coat and punched out on the time clock, it became difficult for her to walk. She had to climb a short stairway to reach the front door and found that to be extremely difficult.

Once home, Mom struggled on the three steps to the back porch. Once inside the house she needed to lay down. Later that evening it became very painful and difficult for her to rise and walk.

An initial visit was made to the doctor. After examination, the doctor felt that she had torn some muscles and ligaments and needed complete bed rest for a short while to let them heal. She returned home and began following the doctor's recommendations.

Days began rolling by eventually turning into weeks and then months. Mom would try hard to do little things but was not getting any better at all. She was spending enormous amounts of time bed ridden. During this time my sister and I had to take on a lot of the household tasks Mom once did herself.

The school we attended required girls to wear uniforms and the boys to wear dress shirts. The task of ironing shirts and blouses now rested on our shoulders. Both shirts and blouses had to be starched rather stiff. Mom would watch our every stroke of the iron to assure our quality met her high standards. Dad was working the evening shift so he took care of Mom during the daytime as best he could.

I personally spent every Saturday morning washing clothes. No, back then it was not just a matter of throwing articles of clothing into a square machine, adding soap, pressing a button, then heading for a television show. It involved many steps and a lot of work.

The ritual started by pushing the washing machine from the corner and positioning it at the center of two laundry tubs located in the back room. The washing machine was a green-colored circular metal tub that stood on four legs containing casters at the feet. The agitator was kept separate and needed to be set into position over the motor-driven center post each time the machine was to be used. A round metal cover was placed over the tub to prevent water from splashing out when it was operated.

Extending upward from the washer tub was a heavy arm that held the wringer. The wringer contained two rotating rollers positioned horizontally one above the other. A large knob directly above the wringer was used to tighten a large spring that put tension on the wringer rollers. As articles of clothing were run through the wringer assembly, water was squeezed out and diverted back into the washer tub.

The washer tub was filled about half way with water. Kettles of hot water heated on the kitchen stove were added regularly to maintain the water temperature. In addition, both laundry tubs were filled halfway with cold water for rinsing the washed clothing. One tub was clear water while the second tub contained a bluing liquid to brighten the clothing colors.

Since our washing machine was a 1930s Montgomery Ward of considerable age and use, a metal tray was placed beneath it to collect transmission fluid that dripped during operation. Once this ritual was complete the wash cycle commenced.

Generally, sheets and whites were done first. The articles of clothing were placed in the soapy water and positioned neatly around the agitator to prevent bunching. The electric washer motor was then started. A lever on the side was pushed to activate the agitator thereby starting a wash cycle.

After fifteen minutes the lever was pulled back to stop the agitator. The wringer was positioned with one half over the washer tub and the other over the first laundry tub. Another small lever turned the wringer on and the clothing was fed through piece by piece. The next load of clothing could then be started in the washer.

While the next load was washing the wringer assembly was repositioned so the wringer sat directly over the center of the two laundry tubs. Clothing already in the first tub was swished by hand and again run through the wringer into the second tub of bluing water. After a five-minute soak in bluing, the wringer was again repositioned to squeeze the bluing water from the clothing. This laundry was now ready to be dried.

Clothes washing usually took about three or four hours each Saturday. Once finished, the laundry tubs were emptied, the pressure was released from the wringer rollers, the washer was drained and cleansed with fresh water, the agitator removed and scrubbed of soap scum, and the washer relocated back to the corner it was stored in.

The wringers utilized in the early washing machines were quite dangerous. Newer models of washing machines had a bar across the top that could be hit with a fist to instantly release the roller pressure. Ours was an older model and did not have this feature. The newspapers were riddled with stories of housewives that were hospitalized with skin torn from their hands and arms from being caught in a wringer. Mom would always hammer this into my head each time I did the wash.

Since washing clothes was pretty tedious, drying them must have been a breeze. Guess again.

Clothes poles stood in the back yard. Dad made them himself using galvanized steel so they would not rust. Cemented into the ground, these poles were located about twenty feet apart and had hooks spaced about a foot apart to string clothes line. Clothes drying took place outside during the warmer months. Before stringing the clothes line, each hook was wiped with a wet rag to remove any dirt, grime, or bird dropping that may have attached itself. The rope lines were then attached and strung one-by-one form hook to hook on the poles. Each article of clothing was then hung on the lines using wood clothes pins and allowed to dry completely.

Once dried, the clothes were remove from the lines, folded, and placed into a large wicker basket for ironing. The clothes lines were removed after each wash cycle and coiled for storage until the following week. Some people would leave their lines up year round. Mom did not. She felt they were vulnerable to collecting soot spewed from chimneys and transferring it onto the clean clothes being dried.

During the winter months Mom had clothes lines in the attic that she used for drying. This prevented wet clothes from freezing outside and ruining the fabric. As she saw it, she had all the possibilities covered.

Days and weeks started to blur and Mom did not seem to be getting any better. After a lengthy process of seeing several doctors, it was determined that she did not have a strain but instead three ruptured discs in her lower spine. She was scheduled for major surgery in 1951 and had to spend several weeks at the hospital in a full body cast. In early 1952 she had additional surgery. Little by little she recovered enough to start doing simple things again. She always had a lot of pain and relied on my sister and me significantly for help.

Since Dad worked evenings they had us kids stay with relatives whenever Mom was in the hospital. On one such occasion my sister and I were split up for a week. I stayed with Uncle Johnny and Aunt Marie Greenfield on Park Street only a block from home. My sister stayed with our Uncle Charlie and Aunt Ida Case (Mom's sister) in Liverpool.

My sister rode the school bus with my cousins each day. It seems that one of Aunt Ida's neighbors that lived on the next street over had a parrot that roosted within a screened back porch. History has it that my sister and possibly one cousin would proceed through the back yard and attempt to educate the parrot with certain slang words that the owner found offensive. Since my sister and I were saints, I found this hard to believe. I hear parrots are mischief makers.

On the other hand, I spent my week at the Greenfield's. My walk to school was a short one. Uncle Johnny and Aunt Marie were older people and it was very quiet living with them. They were very good to me. I practiced my music everyday and completed my homework right after.

On another occasion my sister and I both stayed with Uncle Tom (Dad's brother) and Aunt Helen Overend. They lived on North McBride Street, only a few blocks from our house. We had a lot of fun playing with our four cousins: Ernie, Tommy, Mark, and Dean.

One of the biggest highlights was Thursday dinners. Aunt Helen was Italian and she could cook. I remember leaving for school and she would already be starting the home made spaghetti sauce for the evening meal. She cooked her sauce all day long adding meatballs and steak for an absolutely wonderful Thursday dinner. Moments before mealtime Aunt Helen would send one of my cousins and me a few steps away to Di Lauro's Bakery on East Division Street to fetch a freshly baked loaf of Italian bread.

We were always happy to be back home again. Having Thursday dinners at Aunt Helen and Uncle Tom's house lived in our hearts forever after.

Each time Mom would need to go to the hospital she would come back home feeling a little better. That did not seem to last though. She seemed to have a lot of back pain and continued taking medication for some relief. Many household chores she once did fell upon the shoulders of Dad and us kids. Sometimes it was rough but my sister and I managed to create our share of childhood mischief along the way.

Unfortunately, Mom had to spend the remainder of her life partially handicapped and in pain.

SUMMER OF '52

Once Summer arrived and school was over my Boy Scout meetings were also on hold until September. Music lessons remained all summertime long. Everyday lesson practice was a must. Tuesdays seemed to come so quickly. Even with chores I still found time to indulge in childhood adventures that simply needed to be done.

Sometimes temptation was too much to overcome. One such time boredom was relieved using a small rubber ball. I would honker down well hidden in our driveway. When a car would pass the house I would toss the rubber ball and bounce it off the rear fender. It would be so pleasurable to lie there peering through the lattice spacing under the porch and watching the driver stop, get out, and look around before moving on.

Retrieving the ball required a bit of skill and patience. Occasionally, the offended driver would circle the block trying to catch the mischievous individual. To answer the burning question, no I never got caught. I had to make sure my sister did not see this either, she surely would have tattled.

A careful ear was always on alert for any sound that may announce the approach of childhood intrigue. One such noise would be the roar and hissing sound of a street sweeper. As they appeared slowly maneuvering along the curb we would run to their location, gather together, and follow it alongside to the end of Steuben Street and back again. On some occasions the sweeper would pause at a fire hydrant a few houses down the street, hook up a hose, and open the water valve to replenish the onboard water supply before moving on.

The street sweeper operator must have felt like a Pied Piper. He surely had an escort on almost every street he traversed. Only one thing remained to be done. That was finding a good answer as to what we were doing to get our clothes so dusty and dirty. Unfortunately, there was a cardinal rule about not following a street sweeper and an explanation was expected.

Another fine sound that would attract attention was that of the street washer. Generally, you could hear the engine roar and pressure water spraying on the next street over. This was our cue to head for the front porch and patiently await for the washer truck to round the corner onto our street.

Walking along the side of this vehicle was a poor option. The water it sprayed was very forceful and would soak you in minutes. Also, as the street was being cleansed much debris was loosened and spattered up over the curb.

Childhood nature being what it is, the safest violation was standing in the driveway and on the sidewalk as the sprayer passed. This resulted in a little spray of the water without a lot of debris.

Yes, this too carried a cardinal rule that prohibited leaving the porch to participate in such an event. The solution was to dry off completely before going back into the house and pray that you would not get summoned in too soon.

Our house on Steuben Street had one big advantage over all the rest. We had a storm drain at the curb directly in front. This turned out to be a chamber of treasures second only to the pyramids of Egypt, at least to a young boy. It became a never-ending supply of rubber balls. And, it just so happened that I had stashed away a pair of sticks perfect for retrieving them all.

Once each summer a very large yellow truck would pull-up directly in front of our house and park dead center in the street. The driver and his helper would remove the manhole cover and probe the bottom of the chamber with a metal rod. On occasion, they too would retrieve a ball and toss it to me as I sat on the font step intently watching.

The men would then proceed to the rear of the truck and roll what appeared to be a long canvas sack out onto the street. After attaching a couple of very large hoses to the side of the truck, the workers started an engine. As this engine roared to life the large bag inflated to about five feet in diameter and fifteen feet long. The truck had transformed into a giant vacuum cleaner.

Within minutes, all the debris that had accumulated in the sewer chamber was sucked up and removed to a storage tank on the truck. As the engine for the vacuum cleaner was shut down, the bag slowly started to deflate. While the bag was collapsing the workers would detach the hose, store it away, and replace the manhole cover.

Now, this is where us children would enter the picture. As good neighbors wanting to help, we would jump onto the vacuum bag and stomp it until every last bit of air exhausted itself. The workers just stood by and chuckled at us kids having the time of our lives.

When finished, the bag was folded over on the sides, rolled up, and stored back on the truck. The workers then got in the truck and drove off to the next location where I am quite sure they would be greeted by more eager children.

Before you need to ask, this too was a broken childhood taboo. Being an annual event only, odds of not getting caught were in my favor.

Haircuts were not on my list of necessities but my mother would hand me thirty-five cents and point me out the door and on to Vic's Barber Shop. Vic's was located on Kirkpatrick Street only a few blocks from Steuben Street.

I would walk down Steuben and turn right onto Kirkpatrick Street. The walk would be mostly uphill across Park, Carbon, and Spring Streets. Vic's was located in a two-story house on the corner of Kirkpatrick and Lawrence Streets. The front of the shop contained storefront style bay windows. Several steps led up to the entrance door.

Once inside there was ample seating for at least ten or twelve people. A large framed photo of Lady Godiva on horseback hung on the right wall. The left wall had several shelves that displayed horse figurines along with beautifully handcrafted leather stagecoaches. The stagecoaches were all custom made by Vic himself during his slow time in the shop.

Vic was short in stature, bald on the top, and always wore a long white lab coat. He was a jolly man and seemed to enjoy talking with everyone.

Barber shops back in the late 1940s and early 1950s did a substantial amount of business since most men and boys got haircuts on a regular basis. Even going there on what Mom referred to as "slow times" resulted in being third or fourth in line.

Once in the barber chair Vic would have my hair cut in about five minutes. When finished he would wet it, comb it, and sprinkle perfumed water on it. Then he would chuckle and say: "I can hear your Momma now. She will complain about the smelly stuff I put on."

Vic was right. Mom always hated it when Dad and I came home from the barber shop with what she referred to as "stinky stuff" in our hair. She was always quick to point out that using stinky stuff was probably the reason that most barbers were bald.

My sister and I began going to the movies every Saturday afternoon during the summer months. We would walk to the Globe theater on Kirkpatrick Street. The Globe also sat on the corner of Kirkpatrick and Lawrence Streets directly across from Vic's Barber Shop.

The majority of the movies we saw were not popular feature films. Mostly, they were old westerns and Tarzan films along with an abundance of cartoons and news reels. The admission price was ten cents for children under ten years old and twenty-five cents for those older than ten.

Dad would send us off with twenty cents each. This would cover the cost of a ticket and leave ten cents for a couple of nickel candy bars. Since I was taller than most kids my age, I was always asked how old I was when I purchased my ticket. It became annoying because the questions evolved into month, day, and year after awhile. Once I turned eleven I had to start paying the twenty-five cent price so Dad would send me off with thirty-five cents instead. On occasion, there would be someone new working in the ticket booth. I would approach the window, squat a bit with my knees slightly bent, and purchase a child's ticket. This resulted in a whopping twenty-five cents for the candy counter. Five boxes of Boston Baked Beans went a long way during the movie.

All good and not-so-good things come to an end sooner or later, especially if it happens in the presence of a tattletale. Once word of these ventures reached home the free for all was brought to an abrupt end.

Each summer, the Easy Washer Company held a picnic for all employees and their families at the northeastern shore of Onondaga Lake Park. This large grass and tree-shaded area called Willow Bay was used by many county residents for summer recreation. This specific area was known by the name of Mud Lock. Mud Lock was a canal lock located at the outlet of Onondaga Lake since the early eighteenth century. It provided a water route from Onondaga Lake to the Seneca River and Erie Canal.

On the day of the picnic excitement would reach an all-time high for my sister and me. We would climb into Dad's 1936 Chevy and listen to Mom's litany of do's and don'ts while traveling from

Steuben Street to the Onondaga Lake Park area in Liverpool. Naturally, we both agreed to all concessions and restrictions before we got there, bailed from the car, and cut loose for the day.

At various times throughout the day there were activities such as three- legged runs, potato sack races, and water balloon games. I don't recall participating in any of these games or contests. One of my favorite activities was walking along the rocky shoreline looking for interesting discoveries like large dead fish. To me this was fascinating.

Temporary booths were set up for adults and children. My favorite was the hot-dog booth. Hot-dogs with mustard on buns were available nonstop throughout the day. The secret was to circle the area cautiously to make sure Mom did not catch me violating the "don't be a pig" rule.

Two beverage concessions stood a short distance apart and offered free drinks for the asking. The children had their choice of Royal Palm orange or grape soda. It was absolutely imperative all bottles be returned to the booth when empty.

Parents and other adults surrounded the other booth where the beer flowed like water. There was no need to tell them to return the bottles because many of then stood there all day long. Back then free beer was like manna from heaven. Sweet corn and salt potatoes were on the menu and also distributed in abundance.

A roped off area was fabricated as a corral for donkeys. In between rest periods for the animals the smaller children were treated to donkey rides.

The big event of the day was a boat ride on Onondaga Lake in a powered yacht. The boat was docked at a point near the yacht club. Each employee had a pass for family members to have one ride on the yacht. Dad took my sister and me over to the boat. We boarded and sat along the outside rail in a covered portion of the yacht. The boat would leave the dock, slowly circle to the center of the lake, and return to the dock after about fifteen minutes. Although the lake was quite smelly the ride was fun.

When sunset arrived it was time to return home. We piled back into our old Chevy and slumbered while Mom and Dad got us safely home. We were dead tired, overstuffed, and whiney about getting to the bathroom quickly. Mom's only sympathy was her comment: "I told you two not to be such pigs."

Mom would reminisce from time to time when we were youngsters. She talked about how the canal once ran in the exact spot where the Onondaga Lake Parkway road now runs. Bridges extended across the canal and were used by salt carts to fill the barges that would haul it to market. Mom talked of how they would fish off these bridges. Then she would point out how polluted the water in Onondaga Lake now was.

Dad explained that the Solvay Process Company had large concrete walls on the opposite side of the lake that held toxic chemical waste. Eventually, the walls weakened and the chemicals seeped into the lake causing massive pollution. As children, my sister and I were cautioned to never swim or fish in Onondaga Lake.

One fine Saturday Dad did take us to the lake for a boat ride with his friend Paul.

Paul was a automobile mechanic and had a large boat that he used on Onondaga Lake. He took Dad, my sister, and me for a ride. Naturally, Dad insisted we stay exactly where he seated us and cautioned not to touch the water. The ride was fun. A couple of weeks later Paul was riding in his boat along the shoreline by Onondaga Lake Park. He maneuvered too close to shore and struck a large boulder. The boulder punched a hold in the bottom of his boat and it partially sank in a shallow area only a few hundred yards from the French Fort locale.

Later that same week Paul, Dad, and several other friends all met at the mishap location and proceeded to repair the damaged area of the boat. After several attempts, the task became futile. They all returned the next day with Paul's boat trailer. After a lengthy struggle with the Onondaga Lake rocky shoreline they managed to rescue the damaged boat.

I was allowed to be present for the whole recovery operation even though too young to effectively participate. Within weeks Paul repaired his boat and was again traversing the lake, never again that close to the eastern shoreline.

Coca Cola and Pepsi Cola were in competition for the soft drink market. On many summer days airplanes were in the shy over Syracuse printing and writing their names in mystic white vapors. Initially, the pilots would print the product names in block letters. After awhile, talented pilots actually stepped up to cursive writing.

I found the best place to observe these aerial shows was by lying on top of the chicken coop roof. This was the perfect spot to lay back, relax, and enjoy the show. But, that did not last for long. Mom was very upset each time she noticed remnants of dirt and debris on my backside. For awhile she would assume that I had been crawling through bushes. The fur finally flew when she actually caught me on top of the chicken coop. This now became a major taboo.

The trick from then on was to not show up with a soiled backside. After some thought and ingenuity, a large piece of cardboard tossed to the chicken coop rooftop turned out to be a suitable solution. When the planes were not flying this turned out to be a great sanctuary for reading comic books.

Although we still went fishing on some weekends, Mom and Dad decided that it was time to look around for a more suitable place for our boat. The west end of Oneida Lake was becoming a very active area. The Brewerton auto raceway was becoming very noisy on weekends. Swimming at the cove on Milton point was very restricted due to the rocky shore coupled with a shallow area that tapered sharply into a much deeper area.

One day my Aunt Ida (Mom' sister) and Uncle Charlie Case told my parents about a lot they were purchasing farther down the southern shoreline of Oneida Lake. Other lots adjacent to their property were also available. Mom and Dad decided to take a drive and look at this property. The lots were located along the shoreline of Oneida Lake at a spot called Maple Bay.

The shoreline along Maple Bay was sparsely populated. The western side of the bay was somewhat populated with camps and a boat livery. About twenty-five percent of of the eastern side was populated with a few small camps. The whole southern shoreline was undeveloped. The majority of it was a densely wooded and swampy area. Chittenango Creek flowed into the lake near the northeastern most tip of the bay. A small creek named Black Creek flowed into the lake from the south very near the lot Mom and Dad were considering.

What sold my parents on buying a lot on Maple Bay was the pristine shore area. The water was knee-deep at the shores edge and the bottom was very sandy. The water depth was consistent across the entire inner area of the bay. One could walk out hundreds of feet in distance and the depth would gradually transition to only about three feet. This was ideal for us and our cousins to enjoy many days of recreation in the water with a high degree of safety.

Mom and Dad did purchase a lot with a ninety-foot wide waterfront. In addition, they purchased an additional lot that extended back to a dirt access road. Both lots were heavily populated with an over abundance of willow trees and swamp. Although the land close to the shoreline was dry and stable, much of the remainder was wet swamp requiring boots to be worn when traversed.

The next order of business was the sale of the lot in Brewerton on Milton Point. This lot sold quickly and Dad needed to get the boat removed from anchorage in the cove.

Dad decided to drive the boat on the lake to Maple Bay. He felt that trailering it was not an option since it would be quite impossible to get it from the road to the water because of the swampy conditions. Dad arranged for Uncle Charlie to meet us at the Brewerton lot and drive the old '36 Chevy to pick him up at Maple Bay. Somehow, I had to be part of this six or seven mile boat ride down the lake. I was surprised when Dad announced that he wanted me to ride along. His logic was for me to ride in the front seat and carefully watch for floating debris, shallows, or rocky areas. We donned our life vests and were on our way. As we left the cove we could see Uncle Charlie starting his journey as well.

It was late in the afternoon and Oneida Lake was quite calm. Dads navigation took us along the south shore a safe distance away from all the rocky points that lay between the various bays.

The first checkpoint we passed was Bartel's Point where we then proceeded across the mouth of Muskrat Bay. About thirty minutes into our journey we were approaching Peck Point. At this time Dad slowed the boat significantly and told me to keep a close watch for rocks. Off to our left were Frenchman's and Denman's Islands. Back in the late eighteenth century a road had run from the Peck Point area out to Frenchman's Island. Dad was being cautious to avoid any underwater remnants of a rock bar that may have been left over from the old carriage road days.

The trip continued with the longest stretch ahead. Time passed more slowly as we traveled outside Lower South Bay and approached the Norcross Point area. The shoreline began to appear more elongated as the distance between points significantly increased. One of the longest legs entailed crossing the expanse of Boysen's Bay. Dad again slowed the boat to avoid confrontations with rock bars known to inhabit this area.

Almost two hours had passed as we rounded the final point into the center of Maple Bay. The water was calm as we approached the shore. The pristine sandy lake bottom appeared well offshore as Dad slowly went toward a safe area to disembark. During the last hundred feet I got a face full of small flying bugs. Once back on shore the sun was beginning to set. Dad and I pulled the boat upon the somewhat hollow shoreline.

Except for the calls of some unidentified evening birds, the air was fresh and silent. We unloaded articles from the boat as darkness began to shroud the area. There was no sign of Uncle Charlie, Aunt Ida, Mom, or the ' 36 Chevy. As darkness descended, Dad sat silently and patiently waiting. On the other hand, I inundated him with every possible scenario I could think of for overnight camping in a swamp with no gear.

It was not a whole lot longer when we saw headlights flickering between the trees on the dirt road extension. It became obvious as we lugged the outboard motor, gas tank, cushions, preservers, and anchor to the car that the future would take a lot of work in order to somewhat homestead this property.

Dad chained and padlocked the boat to the nearest tree. I am sure Dad saw this as one task completed. However, I just had the adventure of a lifetime. To my line of thinking, the best fun was yet to come.

Back at home on Steuben Street the Labor Day weekend was only a few weeks away. On many occasions I sat on our front porch steps watching for ants, butterflies, grasshoppers and any other interesting insects that might present themselves in the small shady grassy area between the porch foundation and sidewalk. This was also the perfect vantage point for keeping an eye and ear on the large horse chestnut tree located just two houses away.

Horse chestnut trees began shedding their nuts randomly from late in August on into the Fall season. My sister and I knew almost every chestnut tree location on the north side. Once they started falling we would scour the neighborhood and collect every one we could get our hands on.

Generally, when the chestnuts landed on the ground they were encased in a green and somewhat spiny outer covering. Most of the time this covering was split open slightly and could be readily removed to expose a dark brown smooth-skinned chestnut. A single trip around a few blocks would net about a dozen or more nuts.

Horse chestnuts were not edible. Actually, the meat of the chestnut contained a poison that we were well aware of. My sister and I both kept small cardboard boxes in the back room for amassing our annual collections. Most years we managed to fill these boxes to the brim with hundreds of chestnuts.

We each had large metal steam shovels with cranks that raised, extended, emptied, and lowered the bucket. It was fun digging into chestnuts and piling them around like a construction yard.

Using a pocket knife, I would carve a cylindrical opening on one side of a chestnut and clean out part of the inside. In addition, I would poke a hole into one side, insert a lollypop stick, and pretend I was smoking a pipe. Chestnuts were played with off and on until just about the time school went back in session. That was when Mom had had enough of picking up loose ones that appeared periodically on the back room floor. Although we protested their disposal, we knew that there was always next year when the trees would grow taller and chestnuts would again appear in abundance.

While summer lasted we started making daytime trips to our lot on Maple Bay. Dad had purchased a few cedar stakes that he pounded into the sandy lake bottom near the shore. After nailing wood cross pieces between each pair of evenly spaced posts he placed two-by-four studs length-ways outward from and resting on the shore. He then cut three-foot long pieces of scrap tongue-and-groove sheeting that was then nailed to the studs. This was our very first dock and it extended out about fifteen feet from the shore.

Once the dock was in place the next step was to anchor the boat. For this, Dad used a large galvanized steel pipe that was driven several feet into the sandy lake bottom. The top of the pipe was fitted with a clamp that held a pulley. A rope was tied to the front of the boat, strung through the pulley, slung over the boat, and secured to a post at the dock. This arrangement needed to be robust since the wave action in Maple Bay was much greater than that at the old Milton Point cove.

As the weeks passed it became evident that there was a lot of work to be done on our Maple Bay lot. Trees would need to be cleared, weeds cut, soggy areas to be filled, and the shoreline secured against washout. I loved being outdoors so I was looking forward to future trips to Maple Bay.

The month of September was fast approaching. The time had arrived to pull out the school clothes and determine what still fit and what did not. A trip was made downtown to purchase clothing that was needed. The annual trip to the shoe store closely followed. By the time Labor Day weekend arrived we were wearing our new leather shoes around the house to properly break them in.

Dad was spending much of his spare time sharpening his buck saw, axe, and hatchet for the tree-cutting tasks that lie ahead.

Labor Day weekend had at last arrived. That Saturday morning Mom made sandwiches, filled a glass jug with drinking water, packed some paper plates, and we all headed to our Maple Bay lot.

When we arrived Dad looked over all the trees. He decided that the maple trees would all stay but the willow trees were destined to be cut down. The first tree he selected was what I would call a medium-sized tree, probably about eighteen inches in diameter. Since the buck saw had two handles he showed me how to help him cut with it. Along the way he patiently explained how to check the tree leaning, make an initial cut, notch the cut, and cut the backside to properly fell the tree.

Once down, I found great pleasure in trimming off the top branches with a hatchet while Dad went after the larger ones with a saw or axe. Once limbed, we would again work both ends of the buck saw together and cut the trunk into five or six foot lengths. When finished, these lengths were rolled into water-filled swampy spots that needed to be filled.

Trees this size would take us a whole day to process. On many of the trips back home I would fall fast asleep in the car. The work was hard but I found great pleasure in helping Dad being able to someday achieve his dream of having a camp on the lake.

When Labor Day weekend ended we were all exhausted. There was only one day left before school would be starting again as well as music lessons.

SIXTH GRADE

The Wednesday after Labor Day 1952 had arrived and the first day of Sixth Grade was officially in session. Dress shirts, pants, and neckties were the norm just as they were in past years. Girls had a two week amnesty since they needed to be measured for uniforms.

My Sixth Grade teachers name was Sister Bernadette. She was small in stature, quiet, and came across to me as being very fair and considerate.

Along with the start of school came the resumption of music lessons. It was not long before my music teacher announced that I had progressed to the point of outgrowing my small accordion. He recommended a salesman that arrived at our home with an assortment of flashy full-sized instruments, the cost of which would knock your socks off. After playing several of his accordions, Mom and Dad decided that they would need more time to decide since the cost was quite high. To me, this sounded like another job that needed to be elevated to none other then Santa Claus himself.

Back in school my class work was a little more difficult than the year before. Again, I do not recall a whole lot about school activities that took place during the school year. My memories revert back to outside activities that I considered highlights of that time period.

Within two weeks after school was back in session our Boy Scout meetings restarted on Monday evenings. The first hike we took that fall was to a place called Rams Gulch. Rams Gulch is a somewhat deep valley area located in Onondaga County between Syracuse and Jamesville, New York. Getting there required us Scouts to take a city bus from the north side to downtown, transferring to yet another bus that took us to the Drumlin's Country Club on Nottingham Road. This was the end of the line for the Nottingham bus route and the starting point for our hike to the Gulch itself.

We then proceeded on foot farther out Nottingham Road toward Rock Cut Road. As we approached the valley expanse, a dirt road on the left led us directly to the entrance of the Gulch.

A small wooden shed was positioned on the pathway. This shed contained a bound book and each person entering the gulch area was required to sign-in and record their name along with the date and time of arrival.

The pathway into the Gulch area followed an upper ledge along the northern most ridge of the area. Many large rocks were positioned along this path and hung out over the ridge at the valley's edge. Situated along the pathway was a small wooden building used for a latrine (rustic bathroom facility with all the amenities of an out house). Any Boy Scout using this facility would truly need to

"Be Prepared" and have a paper roll in his backpack. The Gulch was not a place to try to locate a suitable substitute.

A little farther down the trail, two wooden cabins were spaced about five-hundred feet apart in the woods. These cabins could be used for overnight camping if requested in advance.

Since the hike we were on was for one day only, we located suitable areas for starting our patrol fires and cooking lunch. The main activity scheduled for that day was compass reading. The more-senior level scouts mapped out courses down through the gulch itself. We younger scouts used our compasses and paced off distances following compass headings provided by the more senior scouts. I found it to be quite amazing how far we could venture into the wilderness and return using only a map and compass.

The day went by very quickly and I enjoyed every moment of it. Having learned a lot that day, I knew that being a Boy Scout was definitely to my liking.

It was late afternoon when we hiked back down the pathway, logged out at the entrance shed, and headed back up Nottingham Road to the Drumlin's Country Club to catch the bus back home.

While waiting for the bus, we all ducked into the ice-cream bar at the club. Hot fudge sundaes cost fifty-cents back then and we each ordered one. The ice-cream and hot fudge never tasted better.

Once on the bus, I found myself nodding off a bit on the way back into downtown Syracuse. I rode the Park Street bus back to the north side and exited on Pond Street only a short block from home. As I trudged up Steuben Street to home, the old bungalow greeted me like a mansion. I went inside, emptied my backpack, and could hardly wait for the first person to ask what I did that day and how I liked it.

I went to bed early that evening completely exhausted. My head had barely hit the pillow and I was fast asleep.

School was moving along smoothly during the Fall of 1952. Since no notes were going home inquiring about incomplete homework, it was looking like a bonanza year in academics. Since I had a very pleasurable teacher that year, I saw no need to challenge her.

Cereal boxes seemed to sport several plastic items that would squirt water. It became common practice to carry miniature squirt guns to school and create a little excitement during class. Getting caught resulted only in Sister Bernadette confiscating the squirt gun and keeping it. Luckily enough, the shortage only lasted until the next box of breakfast cereal was opened. The excitement intensified if we could manage to get a little perfume into the guns beforehand and not get caught.

I have often wondered how many of America's top-rated double agents may have gotten their best training during their youth while attending a parochial school.

My young life always seemed to be full of surprises. I remember the day that Mom and Dad brought out a small wooden box and placed it on the kitchen table. It had a plastic handle and hasp on one side while the opposite side sported two small hinges. As a matter of fact it looked like a small suitcase.

My sister and I were curious and a bit puzzled as Dad flipped the latch and opened the cover on this mystery box. Directly under the cover was a thin brown power cord that plugged into an electrical outlet. The interior of the box housed several items. Included was a large round platform that rotated clockwise, a metal arm about nine inches long that rested in a holding clip along one side, a round knob that had the words "ON-OFF-VOLUME" printed beneath it, and a lever that pointed to one of three different numbers, 78, 45, or 33 1/3.

Dad set the lever to 78, plugged it into an electrical outlet, and turned it on. Mom brought out one of the phonograph records and placed it onto the rotating platform called the turntable. Dad then placed the metal arm on the outer edge of the record and we all listened to the music.

We now enjoyed the simplicity and convenience of playing records on a new electric phonograph. Mom sorted through all the old records they had accumulated over the years and picked out the ones she considered scratch free enough to play on this new machine. The remainder went into the trash along with the old crank-as-you-go phonograph.

One thing at that time baffled me and that would be the lever on the phonograph that pointed to three different numbers. I knew that all the old ten-inch records we had were played at 78 revolutions per minute, thus the setting of 78. It was not until several years later that we began to purchase smaller lightweight records that played at 45 revolutions per minute. Again, it took a longer time yet to become acquainted with the large 33 1/3 rpm records that would play for thirty minutes or more on each side.

Many times my sister and I were caught and yelled at for playing records on speeds that they were not intended to be played.

Although we would keep the volume turned down low, I am sure that it was our wild laughter that triggered us getting caught violating this taboo.

As we plunged further and further into the early years of the 1950s, the television industry blossomed into a more developed pastime. Talent and variety shows like Ed Sullivan, Arthur Godfry, and Milton Beryle began to have weekly broadcasts. Our old FADA television was eventually replaced with a newer model Sylvania television set. The picture was larger, sharper, and much more stable. By then we also had two local TV stations to choose from. As exciting as this was, Mom and Dad always made sure that my sister and I had more responsibilities and chores to accomplish than idle time for television viewing.

During this particular era a new technology called stereophonic sound was being developed. Since many people did not understand just what this was, a major radio network and a television network joined forces to set up a demonstration that could be exhibited in every home that had both a radio and a television.

At a pre announced date and time one evening, we tuned our television to the prescribed show while simultaneously setting the radio to a specific station. The television was in the sitting room while the radio was on a wall shelf in the kitchen. The demonstration commenced with the sound of a race car zooming down a track. We took turns standing in the doorway while absorbing the sensation of the car racing from the sitting room side into the kitchen area.

After a short while the broadcast changed over to a musical selection for a few minutes and then ended. Although we found this demonstration to be interesting, the practicality of it all was not very evident at that time. It would be many more years until stereo records and phonographs would take their place in the world. In the meantime, my sister and I would continue to amuse ourselves with the three-numbered lever on the electric phonograph and not getting caught.

On suitable weekends during the Fall we would take day trips out to our new lot on Maple Bay. We spent a lot of time clearing the swampy area of trees, weeds, and brush. Dad had constructed a large wood box sized about five feet square by eighteen inches deep. He would place this box on the boat trailer and utilize it to cart tools and other items needed to start building a camp.

Once the willow trees were removed and the stumps dug out, the lot needed to be filled in and graded before any camp constriction could be considered. Fortunately, there was an area nearby where clay could be quarried, delivered, and used for fill.

Mom and Dad had a friend named Bernadine who, along with her husband and son, ran a small fill trucking operation. Bernadine had two dump trucks and a bulldozer. Since they were working a job nearby one day, Bernadine scheduled some extra time and brought several dump truck loads of clay to our lot. Much to Mom's surprise she had her son bring a small bulldozer and spread the fill throughout the lot.

I surely wanted to ride the bulldozer that day. It was out of the question because both Mom and Dad considered it to be too dangerous. All was not lost, however. I found a sturdy tree branch that worked perfectly for poking dirt from the treads of the bulldozer once it had stopped. This was my first up-close encounter with construction equipment. All was going well until my mother noticed that I was getting pretty dirty. Since clay was not easily removed from clothing, bulldozer cleaning time was over.

No matter how young we were, work was always on the agenda. It seemed to appear regularly right after doing homework and practicing music lessons.

One last thing that needed to be done at the lake this fall was constructing a small tool shed. Since money was always a concern, Dad would manage to find cost-effective sources for materials that would not strain the family budget.

Back in the late 1940s and early 1950s many commercial construction sites would build multiple wood storage shanties where they would store their equipment during non-working hours. One such company was finishing up a project on Grant Boulevard. Dad was offered the opportunity to purchase two of these shanties for a couple of dollars each. However, once payment was accepted, they needed to be dismantled and removed immediately.

Dad hitched up the boat trailer, then he and I traveled to the work site. Dad pointed out the two shanties he had bought and parked as close as possible to them. As he proceeded to dismantle that roofs, my first assignment was to remove all the advertising signs from the sheds.

The signs were all metal displays that advertised mostly soft drinks. I instantly developed a fascination for these signs and just had to salvage them. Although Dad wanted me to rip them off, I took the time to carefully remove nails to prevent any damage to the signs. After removing six or seven of them I carefully tucked them away in the back seat area of the car.

The shanty exteriors were all tongue-and-groove sheeting while the framing was done with two-by-fours. Little by little we removed all the wood and placed it onto the boat trailer. We did not remove any of the nails so caution was of the essence to prevent injury.

Once loaded, the wood was tied down with rope and slowly driven back to our Steuben Street home. The boat trailer was parked at the end of the driveway near the back room entrance. After Dad went inside I managed to remove my bounty of signs from the car and store them in the chicken coop. Dad spotted me doing this and quickly pointed out that there would be hell to pay when the "old lady" found out that I had been junk picking again and dragging it home. This was good stuff to me so I decided to take the risk anyway. After all, how often would one expect their mother to look inside a deserted chicken coop?

My new assignment after school that week was to remove the nails from all the boards, sort them by size, and place them into separate tin cans. Most of the nails came out easily but some did not. The nails used for toe nailing of the wall studs were the most difficult. It took several days to get this done and place all the wood properly back on the trailer.

That was part A of the task. Part B consisted of taking the nails out individually and straightening them using a hammer and a piece of hardwood. Each nail was placed on its side, rolled into position and hammered until straight. I managed to complete this chore in a matter of one or two days sitting on the concrete step at the base of the back porch. There were very few nails that were deemed to be unrecoverable.

Dad now had ample wood to build his tool shed out at the lake. He made it large enough so we could change in and out of our swim wear the following summer. Also, there was enough room for privacy if one of us needed to use the honey bucket.

Before I forget. Just as Dad had predicted, the signs in the chicken coop had been discovered and I was again on center stage. Even after pleading my case like a Philadelphia lawyer, the verdict was handed down to get rid of that junk. As I removed my most valued stuff and bent it up to fit the trash can, I could not help but hold back one item. It was a two-foot high sign shaped like and printed like a Coca Cola bottle. Standing directly in the center was a thermometer.

I quickly nailed it to the front side of the chicken coop. Mom took a liking to it and allowed that one to stay. The rest were set out on the next trash collection day and left Steuben Street forever more.

As we would experience, life was always full of ups and downs. I remember the day when Dad arrived home from work with a white patch over his left eye. While he was operating a lathe, a small metal chip flew up and hit his eye. He immediately was taken to an eye doctor and had the chip successfully removed.

Since he had some residual damage, the doctor put some medicine in his eye and had him keep it covered for a couple of days.

Although it was difficult for him to continue working with one eye covered, he managed to do so. Once the patch was removed, the doctor determined he wold be OK. He had no further trouble with that eye.

The time had arrived when Mom decided to remove everything that was being stored in the front room directly off the parlor. Since the room was the coldest room in the house, Dad cut a floor opening, installed a grate, and ran additional duct work from the octopus furnace to this room. The front room now warmed itself to a cozy temperature much like the rest of the house.

This room was officially my new bedroom. Although it was quite small, I did not seem to care. The bedroom entrance was close to the front wall of the house. When entering the room, there was a full-size window on the right side that looked out onto the front porch. My twin-size bed sat on the far side along the wall. There was no closet so I had a small chest-of- drawers that sat against the wall opposite the side of my bed. This allowed only about twelve inches of room between the drawers and the bed. That left a small area in the corner for a kitchen-style wooden chair where I could place my clothing for the next morning.

The top of my chest-of-drawers had a white cloth that my mother had embroidered. A model boat and airplane that I had built sat atop the cloth doily.

I took a lot of pride in having my new bedroom. Everything had a place and I always made sure it was tidy. Every Saturday morning I had to dust mop the floor while making sure to clean all chest-top items as well. Of course, the bed was to be made up every morning before leaving for school.

Wintertime was especially pretty since Mom would place small wreathes with red lights in the front windows, one in the parlor and the other in my room. When the wreaths were lit the shade was left up halfway. It was very relaxing to lay in bed at night and watch the snow fall in the glow of this light.

Although it was well into Fall, Dad managed to come up with one last chore that I needed to help him with. We hitched up the boat trailer and cargo box to the car and drove to a friend's farm where Dad had arranged to collect rocks for reinforcing the shoreline at Maple Bay.

When we arrived at the farm, Dad backed the trailer across a small field to a long line of piled rocks that had been extracted from a farm field. As we began filling the trailer Dad passed me a pair of work gloves to use. I quickly pointed out that it was easier to just use my hands because the work gloves were rather bulky. I quickly changed my mind when he brought up the subject of snakes living in the rock pile.

We loaded the trailer several times that day, taking the rocks to the shore line of the new lot. After the final trip, Dad put on his hip boots and positioned some of the rocks along the shore area that was most washed out. The rest would need to wait until the following year.

As the end of October approached each year, the time to prepare for Halloween created an excitement unlike any other. The first order of business was to bring our costumes down from the attic and make sure they still fit properly.

In my very young days, the first time Mom took us trick-or-treating I was dressed up in one of Mom's old green dresses. I wore an old lady mask while Mom delighted in stuffing newspaper in all the appropriate locations under the green dress. I'm not positive but I believe my sister was dressed like a little old man.

Initially, we were too young to traverse the neighborhood so Dad would drive us to the Greenfield's home. I had to climb the back stairway of their Park Street home with great difficulty. We knocked on the window and Uncle Johnny opened the door. Aunt Marie laughed hysterically as did Uncle Johnny. They seemed to have no idea who we were.

We then asked for a treat. Aunt Marie suddenly announced that it was traditional for trick-or-treaters to put on a performance of some sort to warrant a good treat. My sister and I looked at each other, shrugged our shoulders, and then sang a song about a bullfrog. When we finished, Aunt Marie was still not able to identify who we were.

Finally, we lifted our masks. When Aunt Marie saw that I was the one in the green dress she could not seem to stop laughing. She delighted in the stuffed newspaper effect, both back and front. She thought our costumes were the funniest that she ever laid eyes on.

From there we returned downstairs and subjected Aunt Lizzie to the same show. As it turned out, she was equally impressed.

As the years progressed, we graduated to store-bought costumes. Mom made sure they were purchased as large as possible in order to last for several years hence. I can only assume she used some careful thinking before picking the characters of our costumes. Being not too sure exactly what her selection criteria was, my sister was adorned as a witch while I was a bright red devil.

Mom must have been funning us. We were never that bad. I bet to this day that those costumes must have been on sale at the bargain table. Yes, that has to be it.

As we grew older and began to roam the neighborhood ourselves, we carried Paper Mache jack-o-lanterns that held our treats. Since these jack-o- lanterns had semitransparent paper inside over the eye and mouth openings, Dad was able to provide us with small portable flashlights. He fashioned strips of metal into a cylindrical holder for a battery, curled the back tab into a contact for the battery base, and threaded a small hole into the opposite end to accommodate a small flashlight bulb. We would turn on our lights by screwing the bulb in to contact the battery. Unloosening the bulb would shut it off.

Mom developed her own novel way to decorate our Steuben Street kitchen. Since there was a small corner area in the kitchen between the sitting room doorway and the bedroom doorway, it became the perfect spot for her ghost.

She would start out by placing a coat rack in the corner, adding a couple of pillows for bulk, then wrapping the entire ensemble with a white sheet. Once she had formed a head, she added a ghost mask to complete the attraction. She also had paper silhouettes of black cats that were attached to each corner wall.

This ghost always seemed to appear about a week or so before Halloween while we were at school. He was dismantled by All Saint's Day on November First and put to rest for yet another year. The ghost must never have left the Steuben Street home because he has not been seen since.

As Thanksgiving time approached, St. John the Baptist parish would hold a festival and raffle off turkeys. My parents decided to go to the festival. Naturally, my sister and I were to tag along.

Going to a festival that was held at the school I attended could put me in a tough situation, depending on whether or not the Sisters that taught there would be at the raffle. For me, this was a very chancy proposition. A chance meeting with my teacher might not necessarily be wise that close to Christmas. It's amazing how every little classroom blurb suddenly overwhelms a young boy's mind with untold escapades that may suddenly be revealed. Should I see my teacher, it would be a good idea to to say hello far away from my parents. No matter where they are standing, it's always best to temporarily lose sight of them.

Tickets were sold to adults only and a large wheel was spun to determine the winner. After a few tries at the wheel, Mom decided that it was time to purchase a turkey at the store. After a short while we returned home with a few nickels less. We met my cousin Eddie on the way out holding a turkey he had won. This turned out to be the first and last turkey raffle we attended.

Time passed quickly between Thanksgiving and Christmas as vacation had once again arrived. When we awoke on Christmas morning I found that old Santa had come through again. Each of us had gifts around the tree fence stacked in four separate small piles. Alone in the center stood a large gray suitcase. Attached to the handle was a tag on a string. It was the new accordion from Santa to the whole family.

By this time my sister was also taking accordion lessons. For a short while, the race was on to see who could get to the accordion first and practice our music lessons. Human nature being what it is, that did not last very long. After awhile, practicing took on the drudgery of a chore just as did homework, snow shoveling, fetching coal, and room cleaning. Mom just never bought the story that I could not practice because my sister used the accordion too long. But, it was always worth a try.

Although many families decorated inside their homes, outside decorations were very limited. During the late forties and early fifties many families only made enough money to sustain their family responsibilities. Not a lot of money remained for decorating. In addition, spending money on using electricity excessively was considered not to be frugal. This being said, there were displays around Syracuse just waiting to be viewed.

One such area was downtown Syracuse itself. During the shopping season before Christmas, the department stores on South Salina Street were brightly lit with some of the finest looking displays ever seen. Dad would always select a suitable night and drive my sister and me down to Clinton Square to view the beautiful Nativity scene along with the large Christmas tree. To us this was magical. Turning to face down Salina Street, we could see all the garland stretched and draped over the street from storefront to storefront.

From there we would walk about two blocks south and pause at the E.W. Edwards and Sons department store. Dad would take us in the front door, past the jewelry and perfume tables, and up the elevator to the second floor. Once the elevator door opened, we were entering a mystical area where the magic began. It was an aura of a perfect children's Christmas.

The whole floor was transformed into a wonderland of toys and Christmas decorations. Circling the room was a child-sized monorail that was designed to look like a bullet train or some sort of early rocket. Of course, the highlight of the visit was to sit on Santa's lap and iterate our Christmas gift list, then walk away with a candy cane he presented to us.

Since Mom and Dad always struggled to maintain a balanced budget, sightseeing was the highlight of this journey. We were reminded ahead of time to not ask Santa for anything beyond the desires we had already expressed at home. The parental logic being that Santa had already prepared for his journey and his elves would not have time to add extra items that late in the season. I guess they had it all covered back then.

Unfortunately, my sister and I never got to ride on the monorail. During our younger years we were told that we were too small to ride. After awhile the reason changed to being too old and the ride was for little kids. Somehow we never deliberated together to figure that one out.

As we departed the store, we would continue southbound on the west side of South Salina Street stopping at various storefront windows and looking at the scenic displays behind each window.

Upon passing under the marquee of Lowe's State Theater, Dad would duck into the Peanut Shop to purchase a large bag of freshly roasted peanuts. Each time we visited at least two roasting machines were in operation and the aroma of roasting peanuts just permeated the air all around.

Venturing further south we would pass under the marquees of the RKO Keith's and Paramount theaters, always pausing to read the coming attraction posters.

As we approached Lorenzo's Restaurant, Dad would change direction and cross the street. From there we would extend our journey northward while viewing all the window displays on the east side of South Salina Street. W.T. Grants was the biggest attraction with it's large mechanical Santa. As I recall, Santa would rise up from a large chair, wave his arm, move his head, recite a ho ho ho, then return to the sitting position to start the cycle once again.

Other attractions we would pass on the return to our car were Chappel's, Dey Brothers, and Witherill's department stores. One last stop was in front of Ed Guth's Hobby store located, at that time, on East Genesee Street across from Hanover Square and adjacent to the State Tower Building. The hobby shop had two large window displays, one on each side of the entrance walkway. Both sides of the walkway displayed model airplane and boat kits as well as various size engines. Everything imaginable that related to hobbies was neatly arranged to attract all would-be hobbyists. Dad had all he could do to drag my sister and I from these windows.

Once back home on Steuben Street, I would enjoy sitting quietly and rerun the day's events through my mind. Upon calculating,

I would always come up with the same result. There just was not enough bottles to collect during the summer to warrant a buying trip to Ed Guth's.

During the week between Christmas and New Years we would take a drive out Old Liverpool Road past the Galeville Store. Dad would then turn onto Electronics Parkway (formerly Hopkins Road). We would pass the house that Dad built when I was born and continue up to the large General Electric complex that was now completed. The first building was called the Administration building. This building contained a wide porch-like area that sported a display of Christmas lights and a large Nativity scene. Cars slowed to a crawl so their occupants could all view the beautiful display.

When Christmas week vacation was over it was back to school again. This particular year we had a serious situation develop on Steuben Street. When traveling to school, my sister and I would normally walk on our side of the street all the way to Kirkpatrick Street before crossing over. Then suddenly, something changed all that. About four or five houses from the corner, a beagle dog would suddenly appear in the sidewalk and prevent us from passing one particular house. If we tried to continue on our side of the street, the dog would snarl at us. This forced my sister and I to cross in the middle of the block rather than at the corner as we were instructed to do. This continued daily for a few weeks.

One day my cousin Eddie caught up with my sister and me halfway home for lunch. He wanted to visit with my mother for awhile during his lunch break. As we rounded the corner from Kirkpatrick Street onto Steuben, Eddie proceeded to immediately cross onto our side of the street. We quickly advised him not to do so and explained why.

Sure enough, the closer we came to the house in question the beagle appeared howling and snapping his snout. Being several years our senior, Eddie quickly assessed the situation and advised that the problem with that dog was that it needed a dog biscuit. He then reached down, scooped a glove full of snow, formed a snowball, and tossed it at the dog. The snowball landed directly on the dog's butt and the dog immediately ran back into it's own yard.

After eating lunch we headed back down the street to school. As we approached the "dog zone" there was no sign of a sidewalk encounter. Eddie assured us that the dog biscuit he so effectively delivered had done the trick. Eddie turned out to be correct. We never had a problem walking down our side of the street again. Harmony was restored on Steuben Street.

During the long winter days that filled the weeks until Spring, we enjoyed playing with cereal box toys. Some cereal boxes had cutouts on the backs and sides. I can remember a collection of locomotive pieces that were on Cheerios boxes back then. I would cut out the various pieces, use the tabs and slots to assemble them, and amass a paper railroad station. There was an old style engine with a large smokestack, a larger locomotive, and a small yard diesel. One box had a water tower with a spout. I would spend a lot of time cutting these as precisely as possible. Then, play with them, disassemble them, and store them in a cigar box for safe keeping until the urge again struck.

Other cereal boxes contained small items wrapped in cellophane paper and embedded within the cereal itself. One of my favorite collections of airplanes came from a cereal box. Although I do not recall the brand, I can remember having a cigar box containing my collection of about fifteen old propeller driven airplanes. They were small, varying in size from one to two inches in wing span. All were made of some sort of gray molded plastic. My best choice of runway while playing with these was the window sill in the bathroom. The window was made of frosted glass resembling a hazy sky. It was the only window sill in the house that did not have a curtain that could interfere with imagined aerial operations.

Of course, the ultimate source of small toys was the Cracker Jacks box. With Cracker Jacks, you would munch good tasting caramel corn with peanuts and wound up with a prize to boot. Many of the toys were generally animated characters brought to life in molded plastic with a flat base for standing up. On occasion, you would get paper games, folded trick cards, or even a tiny booklet that would play a cartoon when the pages were flipped rapidly on a tabletop.

As Winter continued on toward Spring, my Monday evening Boy Scout meetings introduced us to preparations for upcoming hikes and camping trips. One time our leaders brought in small tree branches trimmed down to represent undersized logs. Along with this came a large ball of twine. Our whole meeting consisted of learning how to use the twine to lash logs together and form stable objects useful when camping in the woods.

We also studied and performed tasks that we would need to demonstrate on camping trips to qualify for promotions in rank. This brings to mind our first camping trip in the Spring of 1953.

We set out on a cool, somewhat wet Spring morning for an overnight camping trip to Rams Gulch. When we arrived there the rain was starting to come down a bit heavily. Upon entering the grounds our Scout leaders stopped at the office and managed to secure permission to use one of the cabins. We walked in a loose formation and finally reached the shelter of the building.

This particular cabin had a small open porch across one end overlooking the gulch itself. Inside it was a wide open area with an array of old military style cots positioned throughout. We quickly rearranged the interior to accommodate our patrol structure and parked our backpacks under the cots. After our leaders attempted a few outside activities, we retreated back to the shelter of the cabin. Since there was a small gas stove in one corner of the room, we all decided to chip in what we had and cook one big meal. After a quick vote, one of our senior Scouts named Bob offered to show us all how to cook sauerbraten. That perked everyone's appetite.

Once supper was over and the cookware cleaned, we prepared our cots for sleep. The first thing we would do is place a layer of newspaper over the cot for heat insulation and then position our sleeping bags atop the paper. This provided additional insulation against the cold since the bed surface was elevated above the floor.

Since the cabin had no electric lights and the troop had only flashlights, we all were in our sleeping bags early. Then, tales of ghost stories began. Although spooky, these stories stayed with me forever. I had great pleasure passing them on to my children and could probably still do it again today.

The next morning we awoke to a semi-foggy, humid, rainy day. This resulted in an early departure since the weather showed no signs of letting up.

Arriving back home later that day, Mom wanted to know what we did in the rain all weekend. She was apparently frantic envisioning us sleeping outside in tents.

This was a perfect opportunity that I could not pass up. I began spinning a yarn about horrible rain, floods, mud slides, and waterfalls right where we camped. After pouring it on thick, I finally mentioned the cabin. Sorry, I cannot repeat what she then said.

It was about one month before my birthday in 1953 when I received a type written letter addressed to me personally. When I opened the envelope, I found that it was from the Boy Scout equipment area of the Dey Brothers department store in downtown Syracuse. The enclosed letter contained an order form for a pie.

The purpose for them contacting me was to solicit my preference for a free pie on my birthday. Since Dey Brothers was the official Boy Scout equipment supplier in Syracuse, they gave each and every Boy Scout a pie on their birthday every year. I merely had to select my pie preference and submit a reply to them. I promptly completed the form and posted it the very next day.

On the day of my birthday, Mom reminded me that I had to go downtown to pick up my pie. I quickly donned my uniform, caught a bus on North Salina and Kirkpatrick Streets and headed for Dey Brothers. Once there, I walked to the Boy Scout department and announced that I was there to retrieve my pie. A short while later a polite lady appeared from a back room behind the counter with an apple pie. It was exactly what I had ordered.

On the return trip, I sat as motionless as possible riding on the bus, exiting at the Kirkpatrick Street stop, and holding my prize carefully as I climbed the hill back to Steuben Street and the safety of home.

We all enjoyed sharing the pie. After all, the best part being that the pie was free.

Once the month of April had passed, we again turned out attention to the new lot that my parents had purchased on Maple Bay. The water level of Oneida Lake was highest after the ice thaw and throughout the springtime. Some amount of debris always washed on shore. Along with this, many willow tree branches from adjoining lots would fall to the ground and scatter about over our lot. This meant that a springtime cleanup was needed. So, our first visit after Winter resulted in accomplishing this task.

Most of what we collected close to the shoreline was refuse that had been carried and deposited from the lake water. On rare occasions, a treasure of value to a child just might be located. On this particular day, while perusing the shoreline, I found a large duck decoy that had washed up onto the rock-protected shore. With great excitement, I retrieved the decoy, removed the lead weight screwed to the bottom, and took the duck home for safe keeping. Generally, Mom did not allow junk to be dragged home. On this occasion she did not object because she had a fondness for ducks.

After examining the lot and arriving back home, my parents had decided that it was time to build a small camp at Maple Bay. The initial plan was to construct a porch and then add the camp onto it at a later time. The only way they could afford the cost of such a venture was to obtain all the materials at bargain prices. I remember accompanying my Dad to a local cement block manufacturer where he bargained for blocks that had small chips or defects. Little by little he managed to get enough blocks at half-price. He would use his trailer to haul gravel, sand, and bags of concrete to the lake as needed. His idea was to construct pedestals of concrete blocks around the perimeter of the porch and then construct floor joists of wood.

As fate would have it, just before we started construction Dad had to go into the hospital for a hernia operation. After a couple of weeks recovering, he was allowed to return back to work.

Following Dad's first week of work, we were back at Maple Bay. I had helped my father measure and dig the six rectangular openings for the porch footings. Once dug, I fetched a pail of water. Dad then proceeded to tell me how much cement, gravel, and sand to put in the wheelbarrow for mixing. Once the concrete mixture was ready to pour, I chugged the wheelbarrow over to each opening. I remember having great difficulty trying to tip the wheelbarrow up to dump the concrete. Although he had to help me, Dad was very careful not to re-injure himself.

It took several weekends to set all the footings and blocks in place and let the cement harden. With the framing of the floor started, the camp porch construction was officially underway.

By this time, school examinations were also underway. Once over, my sister and I were again notified by our report cards that we were both successful and being promoted to our next grade. School was over for another year, the weather was hot, and another summer vacation had arrived.

SUMMER OF '53

Once school was over for the summer, it never took very long for the eighty and ninety degree temperatures to arrive. During the latter part of June our Boy Scout troop would meet one evening at McChesney Park to practice pitching tents.

McChesney Park was located approximately ten blocks up Pond Street from Steuben Street. Pond Street ended at Grant Boulevard and the entrance to McChesney Park was directly across Grant from Pond Street. Just inside the park along McChesney Park Drive was a grassy area suitable for erecting tents. This was the spot we used to develop our skills. There we could do everything necessary except digging the ditch around the tent once it was erected.

This was my first year in Boy Scouts so I was very attentive to learning this task well. We had a weekend camping excursion called a Camp-o-ree coming up in a few short weeks.

Camp-o-ree was a gathering of all the Boy Scout Troops under the Hiawatha Council in the Syracuse, NY area. The Camp-o-ree was being held at the northwest corner of the local airfield named Hancock Field. This would be at the intersection of South Bay and

Taft roads between Mattydale and North Syracuse. Although vacated at that time, this section of the airport contained several taxi ways and hard stands where bombers were parked during World War II. Hancock Field was a training base for bomber crews during the war era.

We arrived at the campsite on a Friday afternoon, determined where our camping area would be, and pitched our two-person tents. We spent the weekend practicing our cooking, lashing, and various other skills needed for promotions in rank and merit badges.

Although frowned upon, there was always time after dark for a little prankster activity. One of my favorites was sneaking up to someone else's tent and loosening half the ties allowing one side of the tent to collapse in during the night.

I recall that Saturday night when the boy I was sharing my tent with woke me up. He told me that he had caught a snake in our tent and threw it into the field. It was a small grass snake that was probably more scared than he was. While we were talking about it the quiet sound of giggling could be heard close by. Since young boys do not keep secrets very well, the next morning we found out that we had been the victims of a prank. One of our fellow scouts had tossed the little critter in our tent while we slept. Little did they know that I had handled more frogs, toads, fish, turtles, and snakes than they could find in a month.

Camp-o-ree came to an end that Sunday afternoon. We dismantled the campsite, collected all our gear, cleaned up the area, and left no sign indicating an event of that magnitude had taken place.

Back home on Steuben Street there was always a chore or two that needed to be done. It seemed like the older we got, the broader our range of travel extended. This was a convenience for Mom since we now knew the north side and downtown Syracuse area well enough to find our way around and return home safely. Eleven years old turned out to be the ripe age for running errands during the hot summer days.

One such stint that occurred on a regular basis was going to Myers Meat Market. Myers was located on the corner of Park and Mary Streets, a couple of blocks south on Park from Pond Street. Under instructions from Mom to purchase hamburger, and not ground beef, I would set off on the three-block walk to the market. Upon arriving, I would climb the three steps up and pass through the large front door.

The meat cooler was located on the left side of the interior. As I approached the cooler, a kindly older gentleman would always smile and ask for my order that was usually two pounds of hamburger. He would confirm the order as two pounds of ground beef at which time I would need to correct him. He would smile again while rolling his eyes slightly.

You see, hamburger was one-cent a pound less expensive than ground beef. If I arrived back home with ground beef, Mom would have chastised me over not saving two cents on the purchase.

The butcher was not quite done with me yet. My next polite request was to run the meat through the grinder a second time. Another quick smile and eyeball roll preceded the second grind. The butcher then placed the meat on a thin sheet of waxed paper and weighed it on the scale. He never knew I was following Mom's next instruction. That was to watch the butcher carefully to see that he does not touch the scale with his finger while weighing the meat. And, he never did since he was a good honest man.

Returning home promptly with the meat was essential. Meeting all the prerequisites of the trip and purchase was also essential. This successful accomplishment qualified me for compliments at the supper table that evening. Unfortunately, it also licensed me for many other walks to the meat market.

Some residents on Steuben Street still did not have refrigerators. They kept their items that needed to stay cool in a wooden icebox.

An icebox was a large wood box that had a metal interior. Insulation filled the areas between the metal walls and the wood exterior. The box itself was built to look line a crafted wood cabinet. Attached to the top was a wood and metal insulated door that lifted up from the front to open. Directly under this door was a chamber that held a block of ice for cooling.

Depending on the size of the icebox, the front usually had one or two doors. This allowed access to a chamber area with shelves for holding perishable foods that required cooling. Maintaining the coolness was accomplished by the ice contained in the overhead chamber.

One additional feature was also built into the icebox. A tube ran down from the ice chamber to a small pan that sat beneath the icebox. This pan would collect water from the ice chamber as the ice itself melted away. To avoid a mess, the pan needed to be checked and emptied in a timely fashion to avoid overflow onto the kitchen floor.

Equally important, ice blocks needed to be replenished as the existing blocks would melt.

While sitting on the front porch step on a summer day was always delightful, the heat could become somewhat uncomfortable especially during the midday hours. However, I always knew when the ice truck would be arriving on Steuben Street and specifically which homes it would be stopping at to deliver ice blocks.

After a diligent wait, the People's Ice Company truck would finally make its trek down the street. At the stop closest to our house, the driver would park the truck, walk around and open the back door, pick up an ice pick, then separate large blocks of ice into smaller cubes for delivery. Once the blocks were reduced to smaller ones, he would throw a leather pad over his shoulder, grab a large pair of tongs, hoist the block onto his shoulder and walk to the home of his customer.

This was the point where I would head for the back end of the ice truck and wait for the ice man to return. Arriving back at the truck, the ice man would again open the back door and toss in his tongs and leather pad.

Before re-closing the back door, the ice man would look at me and smile. I would smile back at him. Just as I knew why he was there, he also knew why I was there. The ice man automatically grabbed the ice pick, chiseled off a small chunk of ice, and presented it to me before reentering the truck and driving away.

After making sure I thanked him a couple of times, I would head home with my afternoon refreshment switching hands all the way. Once home, I would rinse the ice at the kitchen sink and get out the ice pick to split the ice and share with my sister. My sister and I would put our ice chunks into a sheet of wax paper and again sit on the front step. Licking on a chunk of ice sure seemed to make the afternoon much cooler feeling.

Early every Saturday morning we would load the car and travel to Maple Bay for the day. Dad and Mom had decided to delay completion of a camp porch and instead build the camp itself. Dad had sketched a camp with about four-hundred square feet of floor space and was already cutting and nailing floor joists in place.

If the weather was nice, we would go out in the boat and fish for a short while. Upon returning, it was back to construction work.

The only way to afford building the camp was to do it all ourselves. New materials would be too expensive. Dad managed to work his magic and locate sources of used lumber, most of which was removed form old homes and sheds that were torn down. Again, I would pull and straighten nails on weekdays while Dad was at work. On occasion, Dad would make small purchases from the nearby Bridgeport Lumber Company when a few additional boards were needed.

Once all the floor joists were in place, it did not take very long to cut and nail down the tongue-and-groove sheeting thereby completing the flooring for both the porch and camp itself.

Dad continued on each weekend framing the camp and porch walls. Once in awhile he would work a couple of evenings to apply the sheeting to the outside walls of the camp. By the time Dad's shop vacation arrived the last week in July and the first week in August, he managed to complete the exterior sheeting of the camp, the roof rafters, and the sheeting of both the porch and camp roofs.

Next, Dad ordered locking shingles for the roof from Montgomery Wards. When they arrived, he hooked up the boat trailer and we all drove to he Montgomery Ward store in Fulton, NY to pick them up. Arriving back at the camp, he immediately started covering the porch roof then working his way up to the camp peak.

Within a few days the roof was completely installed. This now allowed us to spend time inside on days when it rained.

It took an additional trip to Fulton for the purchase of rectangular gray- colored asphalt siding to cover the exterior of the camp walls. Six-pane barn sash was purchased for the windows. One-by-one, Dad built window frames, hinged the barn sash windows on the side, and hung them to open like a cabinet door would.

Two framed glass windows were located, purchased, and installed in the west side wall where the bedrooms would be locared. Old exterior doors were likewise procured for the side and front camp entrances.

At home on Steuben Street I had assumed the job of mowing the lawn. Power mowers were pretty much nonexistent at this time. We had a reel-type mower that operated by boy power. Holding a long handle and pushing forward would rotate two large side wheels that in turn would turn the blade that cut the grass. Following the mowing, hand shears were used to trim grass around the house, chicken coop, clothes poles, and any other fixed object that the mower could not reach.

Eventually, I became a highly trusted gopher capable of extended shopping responsibility. For example, Mom would give me a ten dollar bill and shopping list to take downtown to the Mohican Market on West Jefferson Street near South Salina Street. Items contained on the list would be five- pounds of pork chops, a pound of baked beans, rice pudding, a dozen half-moon cookies, and a dozen jelly donuts.

Mom would send me off with a cloth shopping bag, umbrella, and instructions to count my change as well as hurry back home before the meat could spoil. The older we grew the more we were called upon for errands like this. Sometimes it was quicker to walk back home from downtown than waiting for a ride at the bus stop.

In the late 1940s and early 1950s milk was delivered throughout the north side neighborhood almost on a daily basis. Some homes had small doors with cupboard-type latches built into the side of the house where the delivery man could place the bottles. Others just used the back porch or some other designated spot.

Milk was packaged in one-quart glass bottles. The top was sealed with a wax coated paper disk that was pressed into the top interior of the bottle. The exterior top rim was then covered with a colored transparent cellophane paper. Smaller glass bottles were also available with heavy cream in them.

Although milk was Pasteurized, it was not yet available in a homogenized variety. This meant that the cream would separate and float to the top of the milk. Each time, before pouring the milk for drinking, the bottle would need to be shaken to remix the cream back into the milk. Plastic jugs and paper cartons had not yet been developed at this time.

Mom purchased our milk direct from Mathew's Dairy. Our delivery man's name was Bob Mathews. He was a jovial and kind man always greeting my sister and me with a big smile.

Milk delivery trucks did not have refrigeration units in them. The milk was kept cold with large blocks of ice. As the driver made his deliveries, he would reshuffle the milk and ice blocks as necessary to keep the milk cool.

If you have not guessed it, this was another great source for a cold chunk of ice during the hot summer months. Our milk man was very accommodating about tossing a chunk of ice to a couple of thirsty children.

Delivery trucks from several other dairies would make their appearance all week long. Some were generous with ice chunks for neighborhood kids, but others were not. In a few instances we managed to swipe a piece of ice while the milk man serviced several homes close by to each other.

The highlight of the week was when the Netherland Dairy milk man made his deliveries on Steuben Street. You see, his milk truck was a wagon pulled by a horse. The driver would walk his horse slowly up the street from Kirkpatrick Street and stop near our house. He would then place a heavy weight on the street near the front of the horse. The horse was tethered to this weight so he would not wander away while milk was being delivered.

On many occasions, the Netherland milk man would retrieve a feed bag and hang it in front of his horse to provide him with a noon meal of oats. We never raided the Netherland truck since we were afraid of spooking the horse. Actually, we were terrified since the horse moved back and forth causing the wagon to be continuously in motion. After all, we had plenty of other sources for ice.

There was never a boring moment on Steuben Street. One such event happened on a very hot summer's day.

Dad had purchased two new metal trash cans since the old pair had large holes in the bottoms and were completely worn out. On this particular day, the cans were filled, covered, and set at the street side for garbage pickup.

It's important to understand, Mom and Dad were very careful as to how garbage was handled. In our home there was an established ritual that had to be followed. In an effort to control the housefly population, any organic garbage was carefully and securely wrapped in newspaper and placed in the garbage cans.

Now remember, polio was around in epidemic proportions and the cause at this time was believed to be related to houseflies. Therefore, Mom and Dad both insisted on super-careful garbage disposal.

With the two new garbage cans gleaming in the sun, the garbage truck rolled to a stop in front of our house. In an effort to conserve energy or maintain efficiency, the garbage man removed the covers from the cans and set them aside. He then snatched up the cans, walked to the next house down, and dumped their garbage into our cans before proceeding to the back of the garbage truck to empty them. Unfortunately, the next door neighbor took no precautions about isolating their garbage. The odor was something else to talk about.

Mom asked me to bring the trash cans back and return them to the cellar landing where they were normally stored. I carried them to the back yard, asked her to come outside, and showed her the mess that now resided in our new cans. Then, all hell broke loose.

Mom's fuse had been lit. You could hear her complaining loudly as she rushed in and out from the kitchen with kettles of boiling water. She worked for almost an hour scalding the thousands of maggots that were dumped into the can by the garbage man.

Once the scalding ritual ended, the cans were positioned facing the sun until they dried out. But, the show was not over yet. Mom immediately telephoned the city Public Works Department and had a good screech session with them over this mixing practice. To assure the message had been properly conveyed, Mom would watch like a hawk each subsequent garbage day. She did manage to intercept a garbage men heading for the neighbor's can one additional time. I am sure this man mended his ways immediately after Mom's appearance on the front porch.

Houseflies were a major nuisance more so than they seem to be today. They would congregate inside peoples homes to the extent that fly papers were hung from ceiling light fixtures in several rooms in an effort to trap and dispose of them.

Flypaper was available in long strips of waxed paper coated with a thick layer of gooey material that would attract the flies. Once they landed on this gooey material they were stuck and could not release themselves to fly away.

Flypaper came coiled in a two-inch long paper tube. A string on one end was used to attach the end high above. The paper tube was then pulled down allowing the flypaper to extend in a spiral fashion to a two- or three-foot length. It was not uncommon to find over one-hundred flies attached to a flypaper within a week's time.

My sister and I had to use great caution around flypaper. If we accidentally came in contact with it, the sticky goo was very difficult to remove.

I recall one rainy day when my sister and I were milling around looking for something different to do. Mom told us we could use that pent up energy to make some butter. Not knowing exactly how that was done, Mom quickly got us started.

After presenting us with a quart-size jar and cover, she removed a pint of cream from the refrigerator. She opened the bottle, dumped the cream into the quart jar, and tightened the cover. She then handed us the jar along with instructions to shake it until we produced butter.

Since this shaking process was exhausting, we shared this task for quite awhile. Every time we complained that there was not butter, Mom would reply: "Just keep shaking."

As I recall, this went on for hours. Finally, a small wad of butter started to appear in the bottom of the jar. By the time we ended, we had manufactured a lump of butter that was about the size of a tablespoon. That turned out to be our first and last attempt at making butter. I often wonder how much amusement Mom got out of that session.

Another of my favorite summertime pleasures took place on cooler rainy days. Mom would announce that she had decided to take the chill out of the house by baking pies. Lemon and apple were always at the top of the pie list.

I never really participated in making lemon pies. Mom made them the old fashioned way. This required the lemon filling to be prepared hot on the stovetop and the crust to be pre-baked before the filling was added. This was a job for Mom alone.

However, making apple pies was my favorite. I was always available for participating in the first step which was peeling the apples.

For me, an apple peeler was out of the question. I used a paring knife only. Although it was important to get the apples peeled in a timely fashion, I had developed my own personal challenge that added a lot of fun to the process. I would carefully start on the upper edge of the apple, peel around the apple continuously while spiraling downward, and taking great care so as to not break off the peeling before reaching the bottom of the apple. This was a personal challenge that I had developed into an art form.

Then, with great pleasure, I would sling the peeling over my ear and gnaw on it while starting on the next apple. I don't think Mom ever grasped the feeling of artistic satisfaction like I did. As a matter of fact, she found apple peelings draped over my ear to be not so charming.

Like all the previous summers, the summer of 1953 also came to a close. Preparations were made at the camp on Maple Bay to hang doors and windows that were needed to keep out the winter weather. A few items would remain and tended to during the Fall season.

SEVENTH GRADE

∽

Labor Day came a little later than usual in 1953, so school was not back in session until the ninth of September. My Seventh Grade teacher was Sister Ann Miriam. As we walked into class, she greeted us with a stern look. That signaled to me that a real challenge may be in the making for the next nine months of school.

It was early that school season that we would be preparing to make our Sacrament of Confirmation later that school year. Sister Ann Miriam would be working with us throughout the year to assure our class fully understood the responsibilities of being Confirmed.

Receiving the Sacrament of Confirmation is an adult privilege within the Catholic religion. Essentially, it is the gift of opening your heart and receiving the Holy Spirit. Among other things, this allows one to accept the gifts of wisdom, understanding, and knowledge. If properly accepted by the individual recipient, it can strengthen fortitude, increase reverence, and provide a healthy fear of God.

At the age of twelve we were considered adult enough to understand the importance of leading a good Christian life. From then on, we would become well aware that the strength of the Holy Spirit would be always with us. Since battles with the devil will always be inevitable, receiving this Sacrament would seal us as adults within the Catholic religion.

Our course of study during Religion class each morning would continue throughout the school year until the month of March.

Although we received our share of rainy weather in Syracuse, there were occasional outbursts of thunderstorms that could be remembered very well. One such storm I can vividly recall.

I was relaxing in a wicker rocking chair that was positioned in the sitting room near the kitchen doorway. It was pouring rain outside. Dad and my sister had just left in the car on a trip to the store. Suddenly, a thunderstorm happened by and the air was crackling with flashes of lightening and thunder.

Mom's rules were in full effect. Don't open any doors. Stay away from the windows. Make sure anything electrical was unplugged from the wall sockets. Refrain from touching water or drain pipes.

The chair I sat in was well away from any of the taboos. The vantage point I had was within view of the parlor front windows, the sitting room side windows and glass porch door, along with the kitchen windows. Each lightening flash seem brighter than the last and each thunder clash ever louder.

Dad and my sister finally arrived back home, scooted onto the back porch and were safely back indoors.

The storm raged on into the evening hours. Needless to say, the electric power eventually went out. To us kids there was nothing any spookier than nighttime, no electric lights, and pulses of lightening illuminating through every window in the house.

The storm ended very late that night. Electricity was not turned back on until the next day. When looking down Steuben Street, I could see tree leaves and branches everywhere. Cleanup men were working feverishly to restore power to other areas. An announcement was made over the radio that every effort was being made to get power back on in all the Syracuse homes, however, streetlights were to remain off for several days yet to come.

Roads were still wet as we set off for school that following Monday morning. My sister and I were under instructions to not touch any tree branch that was hanging near a power line. Everyone seemed to be in a buzz that revolved around the storm.

When we arrived home after school that day, everything was business as usual, homework, accordion practice, and chores.

It was about quarter to seven when I headed out the door to attend my Boy Scout meeting that Monday evening. Mom graciously said: "Don't forget your flashlight. You're going to need it for your walk back home."

I zipped back around, went to my chest drawer, retrieved my official Boy Scout flashlight and left for the meeting. As the next two hours passed, we had our opening ceremony, patrol group sessions, demonstrations, a roaring game of British Bulldog, and closing ceremony. As I exited the school building I finally realized what Mom had said. I looked up Park Street in the direction toward home and it was pitch black. Like the news had reported, no streetlights.

The door light in front of the school building illuminated the pathway to the main sidewalk. After walking a few feet up the sidewalk, I found myself gazing into nothing but a dark abyss. I quickly snatched my flashlight from my belt and turned it on. Now, being able to see the sidewalk, I crossed and headed up Park Street from Danforth toward Kirkpatrick. The canopy of large trees seemed to block any light whatsoever from above. Only an occasional stream of light from a small lamp in a front window would slice through a bit of the darkness.

Rounding the corner onto Kirkpatrick Street, I could see North Salina in the distance. The cars traveling there appeared to give off a small glow similar to a lightening bug flying nearby.

Then, the trek up Steuben Street commenced. Again, the canopy of treetops blanketed the street with complete darkness. Since people retired early, all but one or two houses produced any light at all. My flashlight beam remained trained on the sidewalk since tree roots lifted several sections along the way.

As I approached our home, Mom had the side porch light on and the sitting room door unlocked. As I entered the house, Mom smiled and asked me how I liked walking home in the dark. I told her that it was fun. I never did own up to how scary it really was.

It took almost a week until streetlights finally returned to Steuben Street. During that time I made sure that nothing else would require me to make an evening trip again.

With the fall season coming on quickly now, it was time to again winterize the camp on Maple Bay. Construction on the porch continued this past summer and the front porch was now enclosed.

Dad had purchased old storm windows, turned them sideways, and installed them for porch windows. In addition, he added storm screens on the outside. During the summer months the storm windows were slid upwards and held up with sticks to allow fresh air throughout the camp. Of course, with winter coming Dad would remove all the screens and store them inside.

The boat was removed from the water, put on the trailer, and hauled back home for the winter. It would rest upside down on saw horses and under a canvas cover in our backyard on Steuben Street until springtime would again arrive.

Once the boar was extracted, the dock had to be disassembled and stored onshore to prevent it from dislodging and floating away with the ice during the next spring thaw. Accomplishing all these tasks would generally take both days of a two-day weekend.

Being that Mom was a nurse entitled us to have a private telephone line. Residents on Steuben Street would contact her if a situation developed where someone needed immediate medical attention while waiting for a doctor or ambulance.

On one such occasion, an elderly gentleman named Rocco fell and broke his hip. Someone immediately came and got my mother to calm him until help arrived. I sat on our front porch step and watched. Someone had brought out a kitchen chair and sat him up in it before Mom had gotten there. This was not a good idea since it could have caused additional injury.

Rocco was a very nice man. He would cook angle hair spaghetti and hot spicy tomato sauce. On various random occasions he would bring over a large bowl for our family. One time he called the house and asked my mother to send me over to his home. When I walked over there he handed me a brand new baseball bat. He had bought a box of them and gave them out to some of us in the neighborhood. I kept the bat at our camp for a long time, eventually passing it on to my son when he was old enough to play baseball.

Rocco had a painful but good recovery. He had to heal completely on his own since hip replacements had not been developed yet.

Doctors would contact Mom and ask her to nurse private duty cases around the neighborhood. Many times she would work with patients that were treated by doctors in their homes. I can recall her staying with ill people many nights also.

Being a child whose mother was a nurse had it's ups and downs. As Mom would put it, Dad had a "touch of sugar" and needed to be tested regularly to assure it was under control. I guess, in modern terms, he would be classed as a mild diabetic.

Since elevated sugar levels ran in the maternal side of Dad's family, Mom would also test me every couple of years or so. Well, this was the time she decided to include my testing.

The evening before Mom would give me instructions to leave her a urine specimen in a glass jar that she placed in the bathroom. Specifically, it had to be the first drain in the morning.

When I arose for school the next day, I headed for the bathroom only to find a large glass jar sitting there. Attached to the jar was a strip of adhesive tape with my name written on it. So, I picked up the jar and began to leave my sample. Not being in the mood for this so early on a school morning, I completely filled the jar to the brim and left it standing for Mom to deal with.

I washed, dressed, ate breakfast, and headed out to school. When I arrived home for lunch, Mom seemed to be a bit upset. Upon entering through the back room door, she began to verbally shred me. Of course, the reaction I used in these situations was to smile and present myself as not having any notion of what she was referring to.

With her lips pressed tightly together, she held up the empty jar. This was the time to politely add that I had not forgotten to use it. At the same time I carefully tried to look surprised that it was empty. Immediately following, I could not contain myself any longer and burst out laughing. That did it. She spat out a couple of additional words, warned me not to try a stunt like that again, told me to wash my hands and eat lunch. By the way, after all that my test came out OK.

In the meantime, Seventh Grade was turning out to be a good year in school. Arithmetic became more fascinating since we were now applying our previously learned skills to solve solutions for actual problems. One procedure that I recall being taught in Seventh Grade has since served me well throughout my lifetime.

We had a Social Studies class almost every day. Prior to each next days class, we were assigned a range of pages to read beforehand. Once the reading was completed we were told to make an outline of all the pertinent points. We then used these outlines during the next session to recap the text of the assignment. Learning this technique provided me with a very valuable tool to take out into life.

My sister and I always looked forward to Thanksgiving Day and our four-day weekend associated with it. Only a few weeks later, our Christmas week vacation would arrive and the drudgery of winter chores would begin.

One event we both enjoyed very much was Dad driving us around the Syracuse University area during Christmas vacation. This area was laced with sorority houses and many students who lived off campus. One annual event they all seemed to participate in was snow sculpture.

Dad would drive my sister and me through a four-block area of houses that had large snow sculptures sitting out front between the home and sidewalk. These snow sculptures were elaborately carved and included dragons, castles, comic book characters, etc. Each display would be vividly colored with buckets of water containing food coloring.

Back home on Steuben Street, my sister and I would spend time building our own display of animals and snowmen. Don't think for one minute that Mom and Dad ever allowed us to experiment with food coloring though. That never happened.

Every other winter season my sister and I would be lucky enough to get new winter coats. Mom would then decide if the old coats were usable enough to pass on to someone in need or not. If they were worn out she would cutoff the buttons and save the coats to sell to the rag man for a few pennies.

Once the buttons were removed Mom would store them in a drawer on her sewing machine. On occasion, we would raid that drawer and pick out a couple of large buttons. After finding a piece of string about three feet long, we would loop it through two of the button holes and tie the ends together. Once tied, we would place each end of the large loop over our middle fingers and slide the button to the center. The next step was to swing the button in a rotary motion to wind the string up a bit. We could then pull our hands apart and back again resulting in the button spinning. The harder we did it, the faster the button would spin and a whirring sound could be heard.

Like all good ideas, experimentation would follow. If it worked with a button it should work with other objects. So, we just had to find out. Cutting out a large circular piece of cardboard, poking a couple of holes, and adding string made it a bit more exciting. Adding cut slots along the circumference treated us to a variety of strange sounds.

The ultimate turned out to be a sink strainer. The strainer had to be flattened with a hammer beforehand. Once assembled, the strainer could be spun at a very high speed for a nice high-pitched sound. However, there was one major drawback. The strainer holes had sharp edges that would eventually cut the string and send the strainer flying around the room trying to hit or climb up everything in sight.

This was not good. Mom would come flying in to see what we were doing, identify the source of the runaway strainer, assess everything in sight for damage, and end the fun for that day.

During the school year my sister and I would always walk home for lunch and then return to school for our afternoon session. After arriving back each day, boys would gather near one entrance and await the bell to signal returning to the classroom.

One block away, on the opposite side of the street, stood a public school named Jefferson School. Each day the students would break for lunch slightly later that we did. They were instructed to walk on the opposite side of the street to avoid any mischief developing between public and private school students.

This always seemed to work well except in the winter months. One young boy in particular always led the parade, had an attitude, swore at our school students, and threw snowballs regularly. We, of course, were under specific instructions not to throw any snowballs back. One Sister would slowly patrol the sidewalk in front of Saint John's to assure we complied with this directive. As winter trudged on snowballs would fly from the opposite side and none from our side.

One day, a couple of our girls' were hit with snowballs and cried. This was going to end one way or another. The next day the snow just happened to be good packing. Several of us boys made two or three snowballs apiece and hid them in our pockets. A short while later the public school boys came up the other side as usual. They were tossing snowballs along the way. The Sister on patrol was nearby and commented about not throwing any snowballs as she passed the group of boys I was standing with.

She was about ten feet away with her back toward us when the public school pack leader tossed a snowball directly across from where we stood. Since the stars were aligned in our favor that day, we all pulled out our snowballs at once and pelted the ringleader mercilessly. By the time our Sister on patrol turned around, it was over. The mercenary had turned into a crybaby. We, of course, looked as innocent as newborn pups.

We boys continued to gather out front each lunch period. The bully never tossed a snowball again. Once in awhile we would put our hands into our pockets for effect, smile at each other, and wait for the bell to ring.

Winter was now waning and closing in on Spring. The month of March had arrived and my class was approaching our Confirmation day. Having completed all our studies in preparation, it was time to choose a Confirmation name and submit the name of our sponsor.

Each of us candidates for Confirmation would now choose an additional name. In most instances the name selected would be the same as that of a saint. I chose my Confirmation name to be John. I did this for several reasons. First, the saint I selected was Saint John. Also, my father's name was John as was my Uncle John Greenfield.

I then chose my Uncle John Greenfield as my sponsor. Each candidate selected a sponsor that was a good Christian individual. My Uncle John fit that requirement very well. He attended church at Saint John the Baptist parish where my sister and I went to school. He was also a kind and gentle person that I admired immensely.

As the latter part of March approached, our class would go over to the church and practice processing from our seats to the proper positions along the Communion rail. Once our positions were established, our sponsors had a separate rehearsal of their own.

My Confirmation took place one March evening that year. My classmates all congregated in our school room. We donned our robes. Boys wore red and girls wore white. As the time approached, we all lined up outside the school building in our pre assigned spots, walked slowly to the church, then processed down the aisle to our seats.

Bishop David Cunningham was the bishop assigned to our parish. He stood on the altar, we could see his gentle smile as he addressed the congregation in general and us in particular. We then slowly gathered in our specific locations along the Communion railing. Shortly thereafter, our sponsors moved into position. I felt a hand resting on my left shoulder and glanced around. There was Uncle Johnny dressed in a suit and tie smiling down at me.

It took several minutes for the bishop to arrive at my location. He would stop at each candidate individually, place his hands on our shoulder, call us by our Confirmation name in Latin, anoint our foreheads while announcing to us that we were receiving the graces of the Holy Spirit.

When the ceremony ended, we returned to our classroom, turned in our robes and left the building.

I walked back to Steuben Street with my mother, sister, Uncle Johnny and Aunt Marie, and Aunt Lizzie. We all sat around for a little while and had cake and ice cream.

It was unfortunate that my father could not attend my Confirmation ceremony. That particular week he was assigned to work evenings. Taking time off from assigned work hours was highly frowned upon. One could easily lose their job or lose a portion of a much needed paycheck back then. Dad did manage to call home and see how I did. He instructed my Mother to go into the sitting room closet and retrieve a package for me. When I opened it, much to my surprise was a plastic model kit for a jet airplane. This was the first plastic model kit I ever had.

As a matter of interest, we were also taught that our Conformation name could be included as part of our full name. If used, it would be inserted between ones middle name and surname. Of course, nobody I know ever officially changed their given name to accommodate a Confirmation name.

My twelfth birthday came on Holy Thursday, just three days before Easter. I remember telling everyone that I was declaring a four-day weekend starting on my birthday. In the middle of the following month was my sister's eleventh birthday. Soon after that came final exams, followed by report cards and yet another much needed summer vacation.

Thanksgiving dinner in the Steuben Street kitchen (1952).

Building the camp at Maple Bay in 1954.

SUMMER OF '54

As in the previous year our last Boy Scout meeting was held in McChesney Park. This year it was our turn to teach the new scouts how to properly pitch tents.

After spending a solid two hours accomplishing this task, we carefully dismantled, folded, and placed the tents into the vehicles provided by our Scout leaders. After a quick ceremony everyone dispersed and headed for home.

Several of us would walk down Pond Street together. As we approached a steep downhill section of Pond Street, the very old Saint Joseph's German Cemetery came into sight. The cemetery dated back into the mid 1800s and was no longer properly cared for. Weeds and grass had grown wild for many years and were waist high throughout.

As life would have it, temptation always seemed to be on hand. We immediately challenged each other to play a game of chicken and walk through the middle of the cemetery. Reluctantly, everyone slowly entered at the top of the hill and headed down toward First North Street. All of a sudden, nightfall seemed three shades darker than it was and tripping over small grave markers made it that much spookier.

Once we reached the center area of the cemetery, one of my friends and I moved slightly back from the pack. On a moments notice we both ducked behind large tombstones and began yelling that a ghost had grabbed us and was taking us away. At that point the rest of the boys started running and stumbling all over trying to find a way out of the cemetery. Meanwhile, my friend and I followed the row of markers directly back to Pond Street. As we arrived at the corner of Pond and First North Streets, the remainder of the boys were still struggling toward the lower perimeter. Needless to say we stood there and laughed like fools as, one by one, the boys emerged. Now, it was not really over until we concocted a scary tale as to how we narrowly escaped from a ghost that had captured us.

With the passage of time, the old cemetery was closed. People interred there were all removed to a mass grave in Assumption Cemetery located on Court Street. The land was then refurbished and became the site for a much-needed grocery store for north side residents.

My sister and I always looked forward to the Easy Washer family picnic that took place each summer. This particular year it was moved from Liverpool to an amusement park and picnic area located on Owasco Lake near Auburn, New York. The park was about an hour drive form Syracuse.

Dad had recently sold his 1936 car and replaced it with a used 1949 Chevrolet. The day finally arrived when we all climbed into the car and headed to the picnic. My sister and I enjoyed the ride since this was the farthest we had ever driven away from home. Along the way we counted everything from white houses to telephone poles that appeared in view on the side we each sat on. Of course, the most interesting scenes were the bridges we drove over and the boats on the waterways flowing beneath.

Upon arriving and exiting the car, the aroma of grilled hot dogs and hamburgers filled the air. Mom took a few minutes in the parking lot to remind us not to be pigs and overeat. In the meantime, Dad produced a small tag that attached to our clothing. This tag provided identification at the food stands where sweet corn, hotdogs, hamburgs, and soda were served. It also was our pass for free rides in the amusement park area.

Although the amusement park was a bit on the small side, they did have good selections of rides. There was a large merry-go-round, a rocket ride, a swing ride, and a bullet ride.

I divided most of my time pretty much equally between the rocket and swing rides. The rocket ride consisted of a simple round structure that was tilted at about a thirty degree angle. A walkway surrounded a ring of single-seat tubular-shaped cars that rotated clockwise at the thirty-degree angle. As the ride would start, the center hub would begin rotating counterclockwise thereby creating an image of tremendous speed.

On the other hand, the swing ride was quite docile. Chairs hung suspended on chains from above. The chains were attached to arms that extended out like spokes from a wheel hub. When the ride started the spokes would begin to rotate as would the chain-suspended seats. Centrifugal force from the rotation would thrust the seats outward providing a nice sensation of flying.

My parents would visit with all their friends throughout the day while my sister and I would beat a pathway between the amusement and food booth areas. We never really made pigs of ourselves but we managed to eat enough to be mighty uncomfortable for the ride back home. No matter how bad my stomach would hurt, I would never mention it to Mom. Somehow, I think she knew and just decided not to comment.

One Saturday afternoon I was sitting on the rear porch step pondering the events from a Super Circus show that was on television that morning. It was the first time I had ever seen a clown walking on stilts. I just had to figure a way to make a pair of them.

A trip down Steuben Street and around the block did not yield any suitable materials. I did manage to find a couple of pieces of wood stored in our old chicken coop. Dad heard the hammering and came outside to find out what I was doing. When I explained, he turned and went back into the house. A few minutes later he reappeared on the porch with a small pair of stilts that he had kept in the cellar.

The stilts were about six feet tall. The foot stops were elevated about one foot above the ground. After learning how to mount them properly and practicing by the back porch steps, I decided to walk the sidewalk along side our house. It did not take me long to catch on. Within a matter of one hour I was walking the sidewalks of Steuben Street amazing myself with how much distance I could cover with each step.

Like other childhood endeavors, the neighborhood fad that I established quietly faded away. I don't remember what happened to that pair of stilts that once provided days of boyhood pleasure that summer season.

As the years rolled by Mom had more and more trouble with her injured spine. More often than not, it seemed she was in the hospital for surgeries requiring lengthy recovery times. Because of this, Dad did all the grocery shopping. My sister and I would ride along with him on Friday evenings as he stopped at local stores that ran sales on the items he was looking for.

One store he favored was a Acme grocery store that opened in a large building attached to a small strip mall. This mall was located in Mattydale where LeMoyne Avenue joined up with Wolf Street. The mall consisted of several small stores that included a Daw's Drug store, diner, and appliance store. The parking area was limited. Dad generally parked a short distance from the grocery store itself. This meant that my sister and I would get to traverse the sidewalk and gaze into the store windows.

One evening in particular, my sister saw a notice in the appliance store window offering a free chance to sign up for a drawing. Three prizes were offered, the first prize being a clock radio. My sister told Dad that he should register for a chance at the prizes. In turn, Dad chose to continue to the Acme store for groceries instead.

After checking out and paying the bill we began to backtrack to the car again passing the appliance store window. My sister switched gears into overdrive and pushed Dad into entering the appliance store where he submitted his entry form. We then went to the car, loaded the groceries, and traveled on to the next store for additional sale items.

The following week it was raining as we left the house for the weekly trip for groceries. After arriving, we headed directly for the front door of the Acme store. When Dad completed shopping, we ducked around the corner of the store and walked under the strip mall overhang. As we passed the appliance store my sister noticed a sign in the window. It was the results from the raffle and Dad's name appeared as the winner of the clock radio. We took the groceries back to the car and returned to the storefront. I had never seen my sister so excited as I did when Dad went in and claimed his new radio.

The excitement did not end there. The next day Dad removed the old radio from the kitchen shelf and replaced it with the new one. He promptly gave me the old radio to take apart and examine.

Up until that time I had only managed to take apart old wind-up clocks and watches. This opened up a whole new world for me. I began spending a lot of spare time, first dismantling the radio, figuring out what all the parts were, and cataloging the various parts in cigar boxes. This led to saving money up to purchase a vacuum tube manual leaping into the new and fascinating world of electronics. This was the catalyst that seeded my imagination and led me to a lifelong career in electronic engineering.

As with previous years, this summer also had its share of hot muggy days. On an occasional Saturday evening, Mom would suggest that we walk to Kelly's for some refreshments.

Kelly's was a large brick building located on the corner of Steuben and Pond Streets. The front of the building faced Pond Street. The first floor was divided into three sections. The front section was a bar room and the back two rooms had tables, chairs, and hard wood floors for dancing. The first dance hall sported a jukebox that played all the latest recordings from the 1940s. The second floor had apartments that were rented out for families.

The evening air still carried the warmth of day as we left our home ad walked the half-block to the corner. We would enter Kelly's at a side door that led directly into the dance hall from the Steuben Street side. Dad would head into the bar and return with a circular tray holding two beers, two glasses of orange soda with ice cubes, and a couple of bags of popcorn. Having already seated ourselves at a table, my sister and I were always ready to enjoy an orange soda with popcorn.

As the evening progressed, Mom and Dad would add a nickel or two to the jukebox and dance. On some occasions, Uncle Johnny and Aunt Marie Greenfield would join us. Uncle Johnny was a great outdoors man. I really enjoyed sitting near him and listening to stories of his hunting and fishing adventures.

About nine o'clock in the evening Mom and Dad would gather us up and head back home. We always knew that sooner or later there would be another hot and muggy evening when we would again walk to what became affectionately known as Kelly's beer joint.

Throughout the summer months we spent many weekends staying overnight at our Maple Bay camp, sometimes fishing and other times working on the camp itself. A lot of items still needed to be completed. The windows needed to be planed, primed, and painted. Floors also needed to be primed and painted. A large hole needed to be dug for a septic tank along with several ditches for a drain field. Small sink holes and low spots required filling to level the whole lot. Also, cutting weeds and grass seemed to be a never-ending chore. A small amount of siding had not yet been installed on the driveway side of the camp. Other small tasks, too numerous to mention, were yet to fill many hours.

The Wednesday following Labor Day zoomed in quickly. This slowed camp work down to a crawl for this season. At the same time school was roaring back into session.

EIGHTH GRADE

With the thought of arriving back at school, I was not sure just what to expect during my last year of grammar school. Each previous year seemed to be a roller coaster of highs and lows. I somewhat anticipated that this would be another year of just school-as-usual.

Upon entering the classroom, my teacher smiled, greeted me by my first name, and told me she was happy to see me again. I could not believe my eyes. Standing at the head of the classroom was Sister Helen Francis, the teacher I had for Fourth Grade and became so fond of. If there was going to be such a thing as a perfect school year, with Sister Helen Francis this could be it.

The classroom setting consisted of a full compliment of traditional student desks. In addition, two student chairs with desk arms were positioned directly in front of the first row of fixed desks. Seats were assigned to each individual as we entered the classroom. Surprisingly, I was assigned to occupy one of the desk-arm chairs in front. The other front chair was assigned to a new boy named Billy.

Feeling a bit inquisitive but reluctant to ask, I soon found out why I was posted in this conspicuous location. Billy and I were called on to raise and lower the American flag daily on the flag pole in front of the school building. Should it begin to rain, our front row seating allowed us to quietly exit the classroom, retrieve the flag, and position it over an assigned stair rail for drying. One of the requirements of being a Boy Scout was knowing how to properly fold an American flag. Our last assignment of the day was to fold and store the flag for the next day.

Within a few days after school began, Billy and I were two of the eight boys selected to be patrol boys. We were each issued a white belt that was worn around the waist and also extended across the front of our bodies diagonally from left, over the right shoulder, and down the back.

This was the first year Billy was attending Saint John's school. Since Billy and I sat close to each other in class and played handball in the school yard occasionally after school, it pleasured us both to be assigned to the same corner located at the intersection of Danforth and Carbon Streets. No matter what the weather, we were both at our assigned location each morning, noon, and late afternoon.

As Billy and I patrolled our corner each day, we would bring pockets of peanuts to snack on while on duty. On one day a squirrel came wandering around the area. Billy tossed him a peanut and the squirrel quickly retrieved it, ran a short distance away, then stopped to open and devour the peanuts inside. It only took a few days for the squirrel to warmup to us and become a regular visitor to this corner. Eventually, we named the squirrel Nuts. Nuts became friendly enough to approach us and place his front feet on our knees as we squatted to feed him. After awhile, we had to stop feeding him because he started showing up with several friends and was getting out of hand quite quickly.

Billy and I became best of friends that year. We played handball regularly and enjoyed games of marbles as well.

Eighth grade quickly turned into my most favorite year in grade school. We had reached the day when it was time to get measured for our class ring. The class ring would be made of silver with a cross and small banner that included the year 1955 on it. I did not know if my parents would be receptive to purchasing a silver ring or not. When I arrive home, Mom surprised me and agreed on the spot.

It turned out that Mom's spinal injury became permanent and left her partially disabled and in a lot of pain. She had had several surgeries and body casts over the years and nothing would ever seem to change her condition. Mom was given prescriptions for pain medication but that only helped her for short periods of time. Generally, she would be at her best for a few hours in the mornings. As her pain increased thereafter, she would take a pain pill and lie down for awhile to rest.

After some adjustment, the pain medication started to do strange things to her. My sister and I saw her disposition gradually change from fun-loving and pleasant to a disposition of frustration and anger. Upon arriving home from school each day, our first task was to wake Mom from her afternoon rest. This eventually became a chore we dreaded because, more so than not, she would awake in a sour mood.

I recall one day when we arrived home, went to the bedroom doorway, and began calling Mom's name to wake her up. Mom did not respond as she usually would. We yelled louder. Still nothing. We could see she was breathing so we hollered even louder while shaking the bed. Still she did not awaken. After debating whether or not to call an ambulance, we both screamed out her name simultaneously. That time she was finally rousted and could not understand why we were in tears and shaking. My sister and I tried ever so carefully to explain what had taken place while hoping we would not arouse a angry reaction from her.

Mom was totally unaware of the scare we incurred that day. She felt that we should have shaken her a little harder. Unfortunately, Mom never understood that we had already applied everything but an earthquake that afternoon.

October of 1954 started out with a warm streak resulting in daytime high temperatures reaching up to around the eighty degree mark on the thermometer. Everyone seemed to sense that this was a bit unusual for Syracuse, New York.

Right around Columbus Day the local radio stations started reporting that a hurricane named Hazel was tracking a path up the lower eastern coastline of the United States. By Columbus Day it had crossed the shoreline down near Virginia and began moving inland. By midweek weather forecasters predicted the pathway of Hazel would extend up through New York State and pass very close to the Syracuse area.

When Friday the fifteenth of October had arrived, the local temperature remained in the mid-seventies. School was out for the weekend and Mom told me to be prepared for a quick supper when Dad arrived home from work. We had some unfinished business that needed to get done out at the lake. Although the boat and dock were already removed and stored for the winter season, the siding on one side of the camp needed to be completed.

The wind was picking up and significantly increasing in speed as Dad and I started out down Steuben Street for our camp on Maple Bay. Upon arriving at the camp, we could see that the lake was quite riled with waves washing up over the stoney shoreline. Tree branches were bending and thrashing about in a much greater fashion than I ever remembered seeing previously.

Since darkness had fallen, Dad rigged an extension cord and hand-held light. My job for the evening was to provide the light Dad needed to complete covering the unfinished portion of the camp porch wall. Much rain was being predicted and it would take about three hours to finish the job.

Things went smoothly for awhile and then the wind speed began to accelerate even more. Before the last couple of shingles were cut and nailed in place, the wind was puffing away at forty-five miles per hour. Shining the light towards the lake revealed that waves were splashing over the shore and shooting wildly into the air about four or five feet high. Many of these waves would cover the ground back at least thirty of forty feet from the shoreline. Of course, I was forbidden to move out for a closer view.

The waves were not the only danger. The lot next to our camp was undeveloped and contained many willow trees. Loud cracking sounds followed by sizable branches breaking off and falling to the ground close by added to the sensation of danger. After securing the camp once more, we finally headed back home. The wind and rain made driving slow and difficult. By the time we arrived back home, Hazel was raising havoc all over the city of Syracuse. As she passed north and headed toward Toronto, Canada, tree branches and electric wires were scattered throughout the area. Much work would lie ahead for the cleanup crews. As we started out to school that following Monday morning, Mom reiterated a list of safety precautions for the walk there. On top of the list was a warning to not touch or walk close to any downed wires. Fortunately, there were none along our route.

Hazel turned out to be a very nasty storm. Her name persisted on the lips of many in the Steuben Street neighborhood for weeks later. As I recall, the name Hazel was retired and not used for any future hurricanes.

As the Thanksgiving and Christmas seasons approached, Mom and Dad began talking about possibly looking for a house in the Lyncourt area just east of the city and outside the city limits. They felt my sister and I were now old enough to take a bus to school each day. On mild days during the winter season they would travel to the Lyncourt area and view homes that were up for sale.

By the time the calendar had rolled into February 1955, nothing suitable to Mom's requirements could be found. They then began thinking of having a new house built. The only property available was a small lot located on Roxford Road North. This lot was owned by a family in Rochester, New York. Dad placed a telephone call to this family and they agreed to sell him the lot. The transaction went smoothly and by late February Mom and Dad were the new owners of the property.

The month of March arrived and my sister was finishing her preparation to receive the Sacrament of Confirmation. By the third week of the month, she and her classmates had completed all requirements, rented gowns, and rehearsed.

The day of Confirmation arrived on March 27th right along with a late Spring snow storm. The temperature hovered right at the freezing mark. A snow and sleet combination fell continuously all day long. There was uncertainty as to whether the service would be held that evening. With over a foot of snow accumulated on the ground, the decision was made to go ahead with the ceremony. I was pleased that my sister had managed to make her Confirmation.

Once the weather cleared and the temperature reached a seasonal norm, our attention was turned to the lot in Lyncourt. The property was pretty well consumed by a lot of brush and a small amount of trash.

Dad hooked up the boat trailer with the box and we traveled over there to start the cleanup. It took several days for us to cut all the brush, load the trash, and make several trips to the dump. Once completed, it looked much better.

Mom and Dad began looking for a builder. One day I mentioned that one of my Boy Scout leaders drove a pickup truck that had a builder logo on the front doors. Mom took down the name, contacted him, and worked on a house plan that he could construct within the confines of the space available on the Lyncourt lot. After many meetings, they contracted with this builder and construction of the basement began. From this point on Mom and Dad seemed to be spending most or their time in discussions with the builder.

The remainder of my Eighth Grade year was passing by very quickly. The week of final exams came and went. On the final day of school, my friend Billy and I hoisted the American flag on the flagpole one last time. We then went to our classroom where report cards were to be distributed.

Upon entering the classroom, Sister Helen Francis greeted me with a big smile and congratulated me for scoring a grade of ninety-eight on my math final exam.

Once the report cards were distributed, our class was dismissed for the summer. Billy and I went down stairs, retrieved the flag, and folded it for storage until the fall school season. We both stayed behind a little longer to help tidy up the classroom. As we were leaving, Sister Helen Francis opened the top drawer of her desk and awarded us dice, squirt guns, balls, and other toys she had confiscated throughout the year.

After collecting our booty, Billy and I quickly descended the staircase and were out the front door in a flash. We said goodbye to each other and headed in opposite directions toward our homes. The following week my class had met on a couple of occasions to prepare for our Eighth Grade graduation ceremony. We picked up our graduation caps and gowns that we were previously measured for.

Graduation day had finally arrived and things were not going so well in our Steuben Street home. Mom had decided to take her medication and lie down for a little while before leaving for the ceremony. As Dad tried to awaken her a short while later, she declined to get up. Dad continued to try his best but nothing seemed to work. In frustration, he sent me on to the school with the idea that they would be there shortly.

I arrived at school, went to the assigned location, donned my cap and gown, and assembled in line with my classmates. We walked quietly downstairs to the small auditorium. Upon being signaled, we all walked silently to our prearranged seats on stage.

Once on stage I began to scan the audience for my family. I spotted my Dad and sister sitting in the third or fourth row from the front. It was obvious that Dad was unable to wake Mom from her sleep. I felt that this was not going to end well that day.

Sitting a couple of rows behind Dad were my Aunt Lizzie Greenfield along with Uncle Johnny and Aunt Marie Greenfield.

The lights dimmed as the ceremony began. After a few recitations by some of my classmates, we were called individually to receive our awards. Our school principal, Bishop David Cunningham, was on hand to conduct the distribution of diplomas.

Since we were all called in alphabetical order, it took a bit of time before my name was reached. As the ceremony reached it's completion and the auditorium lights were put back on, I again began to scan the audience. I immediately noticed that Mom was standing against the wall at the rear of the auditorium. I somehow again sensed this was not going to be a tranquil evening.

The first order of business before dismissal was returning our caps and gowns to our classroom. Once checked out we were free to leave.

Unfortunately, when I caught up with my parents, Mom was on a bit of a tirade. She was very upset and accused Dad of not waking her in time for the ceremony. Since I felt that a volcano was about to erupt, I started walking up Park Street toward home. As I approached the corner of Park and Kirkpatrick Streets I noticed that Aunt Lizzie was standing on the corner. Thinking that she would be walking to our house for coffee and cake, I offered to have her join me for the remainder of the trip.

Feeling tension between Mom and Dad, Aunt Lizzie had decided to opt out of her invitation. As she apologized, Aunt Lizzie handed me a small wrapped gift, gave me a hug and kiss, and turned for her home.

Arriving back home, I opened her gift. It was a silver chain and medal of Saint Christopher the patron saint of travelers. I started wearing the medal from that very day on for over thirty years until the chain finally had seen its last day. And, I still have the medal.

It was not until school reopened that next fall that I realized my friend Billy and his family had apparently moved during the summer months. He did not return to St. John's for high school classes. I had always hoped that I would again see him someday in the future.

SUMMER OF '55

As we slid into the summer months, Mom and Dad were feverishly working with the construction contractor and our new home in Lyncourt was almost completed. Dad's job consisted mainly of sorting through all the things in the cellar that had accumulated over the years. Likewise, Mom was concentrating on the attic and main floor rooms.

One major event involved moving the large wood cooking stove that sat in the back room out to the camp at Maple Bay. One of Dad's friends had a moving van and offered to help him. The van barely fit in the driveway but managed to back in close to the back porch. Dad dismantled the stove as much as possible before attempting to load it into the truck.

The detachable portions went into the truck quite easily. Moving the main part of the stove was quite a different case. It was bulky, awkward, and above all very heavy. Using a combination of wood planks, Dad managed to contrive a way to get from the back porch directly to the moving truck. After much effort was expended, the stove was finally loaded and on the way to the camp.

Upon arriving at Maple Bay, the stove was unloaded and reassembled in the small camp kitchen. This also proved to be no easy job. Once completed, I recall Mom insisting that the stove was there to stay and she had no intention of ever moving it again.

Back at our home, sorting and packing continued. Our music teacher informed my mother that he would not be available to travel to the Lyncourt area for further instruction services.

We were now into the month of July and the Steuben Street bungalow had been sold. Only a few days were left to finish transferring our belongings to our new home.

We all took one last trip back to Steuben Street to walk through the house and make sure nothing was left behind. My sister and I sat in the car while Mom made the excursion within. Without a thought of looking back, we were once again on our way to the new home.

Excitement abounded. Our new street was wider and daytime traffic was minimal. We made new friends quickly. Everything in the house was brand new. A small dial on the hallway wall turned the furnace on and off. Dad would no longer need to haul ashes or shovel coal all hours of the day and night. Mom had plenty of electrical outlets and did not have to remove a light bulb to screw in a socket overhead to iron clothes.

A new phase of life was beginning for my sister and me. We were now adolescents starting on our pathway toward adulthood.

A whole new world was beginning to blossom. High school would begin for me in the fall season while my sister would be entering eighth grade. We were on the cusp of developing the skills that would serve us for a lifetime. The road was to be long but would someday culminate in a career in registered nursing for my sister and electrical engineering for me.

And to think, it all had began with a childhood on Steuben Street.

APPENDIX

Although our parents endured times when it was tough to make ends meet, Mom always managed to create simple meals that my sister and I would cherish even until today. A few of our favorites are hereby presented. The various dish names were spawned by my sister and me. At the time we felt they were appropriate.

GOULASH

Starting with a cast iron frying pan, Mom would scramble a pound of hamburger until it was well done. She would then deposit the scrambled hamburger onto a plate containing paper towels that would absorb the grease as the hamburg cooled. In addition, Mom would clean the frying pan of grease.

Once back on the stove, Mom would start reheating the hamburg, add two cans of Franco American spaghetti with sauce, and a can of green peas (drained). She would continue stirring it all together until it was heated enough to serve.

This was a dish we all really enjoyed.

TURKEY NOODLE CASSEROLE

This dish started with diced cooked turkey. Mom boiled narrow width noodles in salted water. Once cooked and drained, the noodles were placed in a large bowl. The diced turkey was then added and mixed with the noodles. Two cans of undiluted cream-of-mushroom soup were blended into the mix.

Simple to prepare, we all savored this dish.

CHEESE-NOODLE-HOTDOG CASSEROLE

This dish would start with Mom dicing small cubes of orange-colored processed cheese. She would then slice several hot dogs into thin slices that we referred to as buttons.

As always, out would come the cast iron frying pan. The hotdog buttons would be fried until they had a nice slightly charred look to them. They would then be drained on a plate covered with paper toweling.

Mom would then cook egg noodles. Once cooked, the egg noodles were drained and put in a casserole bowl. The hotdogs and diced cheese was then added and mixed together.

The casserole was then placed in the oven to warm. Mom removed it periodically to mix as the chess proceeded to melt and blend in.

Once heated, we all enjoyed this dish.

POTATO PANCAKES

I believe our most favorite of all was Mom's potato pancakes. The recipe for this came from Poland with Mom's great grandmother. Although never written down, it has been passed along orally among the members of Mom's family.

It all begins with peeling the potatoes and that job fell to my sister and me. Each peeled potato was dropped into a bowl of water to minimize exposure to the air. This would prevent discoloration of the potato.

Once peeled, the next step was grating the potatoes. This was accomplished using the course shred side of a simple box grater. This task wad tedious.

Once grating was completed, a large spoon was used to remove excess water from the grated potatoes. Mom would then stir in a small amount of baking powder and salt. In addition, she would add no more that a cup of flower.

Then, out came the cast iron frying pan. Mom would heat a generous amount of shortening deep enough to float the frying pancakes.

A large spoon was then used to ladle the potato pancake mixture into the hot shortening. Generally, the frying pan would hold four at a time. Initially, the batter would sink to the bottom. After a couple of minutes of frying, a common kitchen fork was slid under each pancake to release them from sticking to the frying pan bottom. Each pancake would then float allowing them to be rotated and flipped as necessary.

Once fried, Mom would drain them on a platter covered with paper towels and continue on with the next batch.

Although my sister and I enjoyed ours with clear syrup, Mom and Dad preferred the flavor of maple instead. It was a lot of hard work but the reward was fantastic.

Made in the USA
Middletown, DE
10 January 2021